COMPANY MINUTES
& RESOLUTIONS
MADE EASY

LAWPACK

Company Minutes & Resolutions Made Easy

Copyright 1999 Law Pack Publishing Limited

LAWPACK

10-16 Cole Street London SE1 4YH
www.lawpack.co.uk

ISBN 1 902646 41 X

Table of contents

Section A

How *Company Minutes & Resolutions Made Easy* can help you

What you'll find in this section:

➡ Why good company records are essential

➡ Forming and running a company

➡ Rules affecting directors

➡ Conduct of board meetings

➡ How to use Company Minutes & Resolutions Made Easy

Why good company records are essential

No business owner has become wealthy simply by keeping good company records. But good company record keeping is essential for several important reasons.

DEFINITION

When a company is created you create a legal entity separate and distinct from its shareholders: it has a 'separate corporate personality'. This means that the company makes contracts on its own behalf; its assets are owned by the company; and it can sue and be sued in its own name, (not the shareholders'). Because of this concept of a separate personality the directors and shareholders are, generally, not liable for the actions of the company. Directors can, however, be personally liable for things they have or have not done. For example, where they give personal guarantees or where they are guilty of wrongful or fraudulent trading, or fail to attend to certain obligatory procedures.

Normally a shareholder is liable only for the amount he has paid for his shares. If a shareholder subscribes £1,000 for one thousand £1 shares and the company becomes insolvent owing millions of pounds in debts, the most he can lose is £1,000. Shareholders, like directors, can also be made liable if they are party to fraudulent trading. If your company

note If a shareholder subscribes £1,000 for one thousand £1 shares and the company becomes insolvent owing millions of pounds in debts, the most he can lose is £1,000.

has many shareholders, the need for detailed company records is critical. Any one shareholder may challenge the authority of a decision or transaction. Only complete and accurate resolutions can verify that the action was properly authorised by the directors and/or the shareholders.

CAUTION

If you are a director of a company you should insist on accurate minutes of board meetings so that, if need be, you can prove your actions at these meetings and also show how you voted. Legal actions against directors are becoming more common and you must be able to defend yourself.

Forming a company

Company Minutes & Resolutions Made Easy does not deal with setting up a limited company. This subject is covered by the *Limited Company Formation Made Easy*. However as the articles of association of smaller companies often follow the standard form of Table A of the Companies Act 1985, a copy of this is reproduced in Appendix 2 for convenient reference. In *Company Minutes & Resolutions Made Easy* you will also find a large selection of special resolutions which may be useful if you want to amend the articles of your company.

See forms C34-43 and E39-48 for resolutions to use for amending the articles of your company.

Running a company

The day-to-day control of a company is vested in its directors. A director may be either executive or non-executive. Generally executive directors work full-time for the company and are employed under a service agreement; non-executive directors are part-time and may have a short engagement letter describing what they are to do and how they are paid.

The board of directors will appoint certain officers, typically:

A chairman who chairs board meetings and, unless the articles say otherwise, has a casting vote. He may be executive or non-executive.

A managing director or chief executive who will be executive and responsible for the day- to-day management.

A company secretary, who may or may not be a director, and has responsibility for compliance with formalities such as filing at Companies House and keeping the company's statutory books.

The precise function of the officers and other directors will vary according to the company's requirements and the individuals' abilities. Executives should always have written service agreements clearly defining their role and the other terms on which they are employed; it is also desirable to record the key features of the engagement of any non-executive director.

The statutory books comprise various sections known as registers, e.g. register of members, of directors, of directors' interests in the shares of the company and the register of charges created by the company over its assets (see specimen templates on page 155). Statutory books also include minutes of directors and shareholders meetings or signed resolutions. They should be kept at the company's registered office, available for inspection by the auditors; they will form the basis for preparing the annual return which must be sent each year to Companies House. Employment law is covered in more depth in *Employment Law Made Easy.*

Rules affecting directors

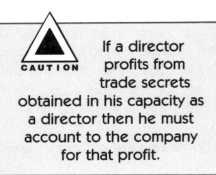

If a director profits from trade secrets obtained in his capacity as a director then he must account to the company for that profit.

The powers of the directors are derived from the company's memorandum and articles of association and general company law. Their powers are extensive and it is for this reason that certain duties and restrictions are imposed on them. For example:

- a director is not allowed to make a personal profit from his position.

- a director must not exceed the power given to him; he must act in good faith in the interests of the company.

- a director owes a duty of care and skill and has to meet a certain standard dependent on his knowledge and experience.

- directors cannot pay an outgoing director a 'golden handshake' without the approval of the shareholders.

- a director cannot be granted a service contract of over five years without the approval of the shareholders.

- with certain exceptions, loans to directors are unlawful.

Conduct of board meetings

CAUTION

The directors exercise their power by voting collectively at board meetings or by signing written resolutions. Certain formalities must be complied with in the running of board meetings. For example:

- a board meeting must be called on reasonable notice. What is reasonable depends on the subject matter of the proposed meeting. The notice does not have to be in writing.

- unless the articles provide otherwise each director has one vote. All resolutions are passed by a majority.

- the articles will specify a minimum number of directors who must be present in person or by their alternate in order for a meeting to be valid. Under Table A this 'quorum' is two, but another number may be substituted.

- minutes must be written up after every meeting and inserted into the appropriate register.

Shareholders' rights

The rights of the shareholders (or 'members') are governed by the articles and by the general law. A simple company will have just one class of shares, probably described as ordinary shares.

The rights usually enjoyed by shareholders include:

(a)   to attend and vote at general meetings, i.e. meetings of the shareholders;

(b)   to receive dividends if declared;

(c)   to receive a distribution of capital on a winding-up.

> note
> A complicated share structure may include 'preference' shares or 'deferred' shares or other designated classes with different rights.

Typically an ordinary shareholder has all three rights, but a holder of preference shares may not have a vote or a right to participate in capital profits on a winding up. The 'preference' usually refers to a right to a fixed dividend and a fixed repayment on a winding up in priority to the ordinary shareholders.

Certain minimum percentages of voting shares are required to take particular steps of which the most important are:

% required	In order to
75	Pass a special resolution
over 50	Pass an ordinary resolution
10	Demand a poll
10	Require the board to convene an EGM

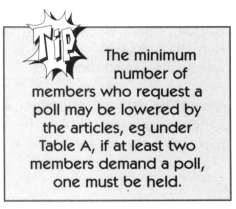

The minimum number of members who request a poll may be lowered by the articles, eg under Table A, if at least two members demand a poll, one must be held.

Votes at shareholders' meetings are normally cast by a show of hands when each shareholder has one vote. However, the chairman may, and if at least five1 members or the holders of at least 10% of the shares represented at the meeting so request he must, order a poll. Votes are then counted according to the numbers of shares held rather than the number of shareholders present at the meeting. Absent shareholders may appoint proxies to represent them according to the articles. Corporate shareholders must appoint a representative to attend which is strictly not the same as a proxy and requires a slightly different form of appointment.

Notice of shareholder meetings

Notice of general meetings of shareholders must be in writing. The amount of notice depends on the type of meeting and the resolution being proposed:

Extraordinary General Meeting (EGM)   Special Resolution: 21 clear days
                                        Ordinary Resolution: 14 clear days

Annual General Meeting (AGM)   21 clear days

Any meeting where a director   21 clear days
    is being appointed

Any meeting where a director   Must leave formal written notice at
    is being removed   registered office at least 28 days
                                        before meeting

It is possible to call a meeting on short notice. For an AGM, the decision to call on short notice must be unanimous. For an EGM, a majority in numbers must agree. That majority must hold at least 95% of all the shares.

For a resolution to be validly passed the meeting must be quorate. As mentioned above, under Table A the requirement is two. This can be increased if the articles are altered. It cannot generally be decreased unless it is a one-member company.

Minutes must be written up and signed by the chairman after every meeting.

How to use Company Minutes & Resolutions Made Easy

Using *Company Minutes & Resolutions Made Easy* is straightforward by following the steps below.

1 Decisions on the running of a company are made by passing resolutions. When questions arise for decision, ask yourself if it is a matter for the directors? If so, do they require a meeting? If yes, go to Section B which contains standard forms for minutes and examples to show you how they are to be completed.

2 If instead they are agreed that it is simply a matter of signing a written resolution go to Section C. The forms for written board resolutions are set out in full in this section; you may wish to combine two or more resolutions from these forms when there is more than one matter to be decided.

3 Alternatively, if the decision is one for the shareholders, does it require a special resolution or an ordinary resolution; and can it dealt with by a signed resolution or is a meeting required? If a meeting is required, go to Section D where you will find the form of notice to be sent to shareholders, minutes and a number of other forms which may be relevant. If, on the other hand, the written resolution procedure may be used, go to Section E where you will find example resolutions contained in an appropriate form and on page 99 detailed instructions on their use. When meetings are needed, you should pay careful attention to the requirements for notice, a quorum at the meeting and voting. In the case of written resolutions,

> *note* The material in Company Minutes & Resolutions Made Easy can be used by any private company of any size. It is not suitable for public limited companies or those listed on the Stock Exchange.

notice and quorum do not apply but you must obtain all the necessary signatures and the resolution is not valid until this has been done.

4 Consult the contents pages of *Company Minutes & Resolutions Made Easy* to see which resolutions can be passed by directors and those which have to be passed by members as special or ordinary resolutions. Company Secretary resolutions have been drafted as directors' written resolutions or standard written resolutions of members, i.e. drafted for use without meetings having to be held by the board or by members. If required the actual resolution wording can be inserted into the Standard Minutes of Board Meetings or of Members' Meetings.

5 Cut out and photocopy the form you want and keep the original so it can be used again in the future. Alternatively, you can use the form as a template to prepare your own documents, especially when you want to combine more than one resolution in one document.

6 Complete each form fully. Make certain all blanks (name, address, dates, amounts) are filled in. You may need to delete or add provisions in some forms to suit your requirements. If this is necessary, make sure each deletion or insertion is initialled by all parties. If there is not enough space on the document to make your insertion, it is best to type out the entire document, including the insertion, on a new sheet of paper.

7 Some forms have footnotes which should be observed if you are to use the form properly. Some forms refer to others in *Company Minutes & Resolutions Made Easy*, copies of documents which will need to be attached to the form before use or Companies House forms available from Companies House at the following address:

Companies House
Crown Way
Cardiff CF4 3UZ
Tel. 01222 388588

8 The aim of *Company Minutes & Resolutions Made Easy* is to be as simple to follow as possible. That means it cannot deal with every set of circumstances which may arise, or list every step you may need to take to comply with company law. If you have any doubt about what to do, you should always take professional advice from the company's lawyers or accountants.

Company decision-making process

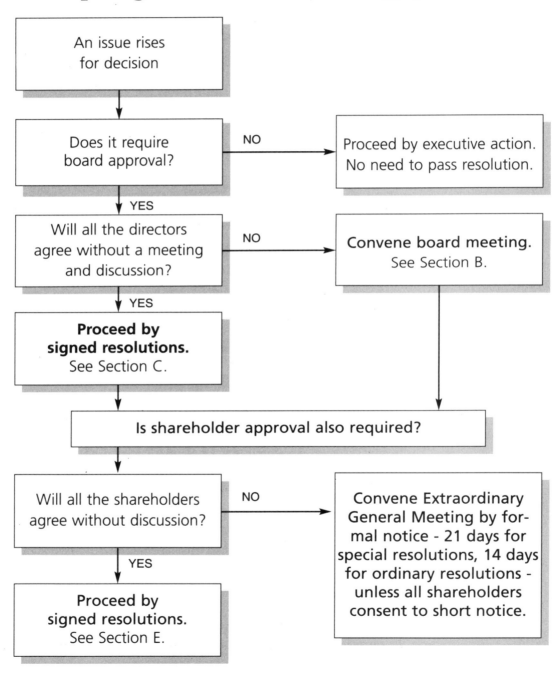

An issue rises
for decision

Does it require
board approval? — NO → Proceed by executive action. No need to pass resolution.

YES

Will all the directors
agree without a meeting
and discussion? — NO → Convene board meeting. See Section B.

YES

**Proceed by
signed resolutions.**
See Section C.

Is shareholder approval also required?

Will all the shareholders
agree without discussion? — NO → Convene Extraordinary General Meeting by formal notice - 21 days for special resolutions, 14 days for ordinary resolutions - unless all shareholders consent to short notice.

YES

**Proceed by
signed resolutions.**
See Section E.

Section B

Board Meetings

What you'll find in this section:

⟹   Minutes of board meetings

Board meetings

When an issue arises for decision relating to a company, first ask yourself whether it requires board approval. It is beyond the scope of *Company Minutes & Resolutions Made Easy* to provide an exhaustive list of such issues; but some examples are: the approval of important contracts to be entered into, the approval of transfers of shares in the company, the allotment of shares (although the directors must have the necessary authority to do this), the approval of the company's accounts and the changing of the company's registered office. If you decide that a board resolution is required but all the directors will agree without discussion, proceed by written resolution - see Section C onwards. However, if you need a board resolution but it also requires a meeting to discuss the issue, use the forms in this section. In addition, certain matters will require the approval of the company's shareholders in which case the directors should pass a resolution calling a general meeting or proposing a written resolution to deal with the issue in question (examples of these kinds of resolutions are also included in

Section C).The text of the actual resolution you require can be selected from those in Section C and then be inserted into the board minutes as appropriate.Where a document is referred to as being attached to the written resolution this should be replaced in the resolution in minute form by reference to the relevant document being 'produced at the meeting'.

Steps to be taken for holding board meetings:

1 Give all the directors proper notice of the meeting. There is no fixed period and in an emergency a meeting may be convened at once but generally allow as much time as is reasonably possible.

2 When the meeting begins, ensure that a quorum is present.

3 When the meeting is concluded, prepare minutes and have them signed by the chairman and filed in the minute book.

4 Consider whether any matter requires to be notified to Companies House or the auditors and, if so, attend to it. Notes on the forms will assist in identifying when this is necessary but they should not be taken to be exhaustive.

Section contents

B01   Notice of board meeting—Announces to all company directors the time, place and agenda of an upcoming board meeting.

B02   Notice of appointment of alternate director—to be given to the secretary by a director who appoints an alternate.A form of resolution approving the appointment is at C11.An alternate may require board approval under the Articles and cannot attend meetings until notice of the appointment has been given. A director may attend meetings himself instead of an alternate.

B03   Minutes of First Board Meeting—a number of routine matters must be attended to at the first meeting of directors following incorporation.

B04   Example Minutes of First Board Meeting—for guidance when completing form B03, typical details have been inserted in this example.

B05   Standard board minutes—all minutes of board meetings must set out the date, time and place of the meeting and who has attended. Those who are directors are shown as 'present' and anyone else as 'in attendance'. Select the resolutions you require from those set out in Section C.

B06   Example Board Minutes—to illustrate how to use Form B05, typical details have been inserted in this example

_____ **LIMITED**

Notice is hereby given[1] that a meeting of the directors of the company will be held at _____ on _____ at _____ a.m./p.m. at which your attendance is requested.

AGENDA

_____

_____

_____

_____

_____

_____

1. Apologies for absence

_____

_____

_____

_____

2. Approval of minutes of last board meeting held on _____

3. _____

_____

_____

_____

4. _____

_____

_____

_____

Signed: _____ Dated: _____

[1]*Must be called on reasonable notice*

Form B01

_____ LIMITED

The Directors

_____

_____

_____

_____

I hereby give notice that I have appointed _____

of _____

_____

to be my alternate director. I hereby request that the board approves this appointment.[1]

Signed: _____ Dated: _____

[1]*Check articles - may not need board approval.*

_____ LIMITED

MINUTES of the first Meeting of the Board of Directors held at
_____ on _____ at _____ a.m./p.m.

PRESENT:

_____
_____
_____

IN ATTENDANCE:

_____
_____
_____

1. The Chairman confirmed that notice of the meeting had been given to all the directors of the Company and that a quorum of the board of directors was present at the meeting.

2. The Chairman reported that the Company had been incorporated on _____ and produced the certificate of incorporation and a print of the memorandum and articles of Association of the Company as filed at the Companies Registry.

3. It was noted that pursuant to Section 10 of the Companies Act 1985 the first Directors of the Company are _____
_____
and its first Secretary is _____.

4. It was further noted that the registered office of the Company was situated at _____

5. IT WAS RESOLVED that _____ be appointed auditors to the Company to act as such until the conclusion of the first annual general meeting of the Company and that their remuneration be at a rate to be subsequently agreed.

6. IT WAS RESOLVED that the accounts of the Company be made up to _____ each year.[1]

7. IT WAS RESOLVED that _____ Bank Plc, _____ branch be appointed bankers of the Company and that the resolutions set out on the form of mandate produced to the meeting (a copy of which is annexed hereto) be approved and passed and deemed to be set out herein in extenso.

[1]This is the company's annual accounting reference date. It is set automatically on the last day of the month in which the anniversary of the company's incorporation falls. This resolution is therefore only needed if the directors wish to change this date. A company's first accounting reference date must be between six and 18 months from the date of incorporation.

[8. IT WAS RESOLVED that the seal produced to the meeting, an impression of which is affixed to these Minutes, be approved and adopted as the common seal of the Company and that it be kept in safe custody by the Secretary.] [2]

9. The Chairman reported the receipt of the sum of £2 representing payment in full for the shares subscribed for by the subscribers to the memorandum of association. [It was noted that the subscribers had waived their rights to share certificates.][3] IT WAS RESOLVED that the names of the subscribers be entered in the register of members in respect of such shares.

10. There were produced to and considered by the meeting the following transfers of shares [with supporting certificates]:
Transferor: _____ Transferee: _____ No. of shares: _____
Transferor: _____ Transferee: _____ No. of shares: _____

11. IT WAS RESOLVED that:
   a. subject to their being represented duly stamped, such transfers be approved;
   b. the names of the transferees be entered in the register of members in respect of the shares transferred to them; and
   c. the Secretary be instructed to prepare share certificates in respect of the shares transferred and to deliver them to the transferees.

12. The Secretary was instructed to arrange for a nameplate to be ordered and affixed outside the registered office.

13. The Secretary was instructed to file Form 225 (accounting reference date) with the registrar of companies.[4]

14. IT WAS RESOLVED that the Company should trade under the name

_____ .
The Secretary was instructed to ensure compliance with the statutory disclosure requirements in the Business Names Act 1985.

15. The payment of the fees incurred in respect of the formation of the company was approved.

16. The Secretary was instructed to register the company with HM Customs & Excise for the purposes of VAT and to supply particulars to the Inland Revenue for tax purposes.

17. There being no other business the meeting ended.

Chairman: _____

[2] A seal is no longer a requirement.
[3] Include only where the subscribers are to transfer their shares immediately.
[4] Include only if accounting reference date has been changed.

Law Pack Publishing **LIMITED**

MINUTES of the first Meeting of the Board of Directors held at
2 James Road, London, SE1 on _Mon 2nd Sept 1999_ at _10.00_ a.m./p.m.

PRESENT:

James Etheridge (in the chair)

Peggy Flanagan

Russell Coles

IN ATTENDANCE:

Caroline Dore

1. The Chairman confirmed that notice of the meeting had been given to all the directors of the Company and that a quorum of the board of directors was present at the meeting.

2. The Chairman reported that the Company had been incorporated on _Wednesday 27 October 1999_ and produced the certificate of incorporation and a print of the memorandum and articles of Association of the Company as filed at the Companies Registry.

3. It was noted that pursuant to Section 10 of the Companies Act 1985 the first Directors of the Company are _James Etheridge_ _Peggy Flanagan_ _Russell Coles_ and its first Secretary is _James Etheridge_ .

4. It was further noted that the registered office of the Company was situated at _2 James Road, London, SE1_

5. IT WAS RESOLVED that _John Ross & Company_ be appointed auditors to the Company to act as such until the conclusion of the first annual general meeting of the Company and that their remuneration be at a rate to be subsequently agreed.

6. IT WAS RESOLVED that the accounts of the Company be made up to _31st March_ each year.[1]

7. IT WAS RESOLVED that _Westminster_ Bank Plc, _Southwark_ branch be appointed bankers of the Company and that the resolutions set out on the form of mandate produced to the meeting (a copy of which is annexed hereto) be approved and passed and deemed to be set out herein in extenso.

[8. IT WAS RESOLVED that the seal produced to the meeting, an impression of which is affixed to these Minutes, be approved and adopted as the common seal of the Company and that it be kept in safe custody by the Secretary.] [2]

9. The Chairman reported the receipt of the sum of £2 representing payment in full for the shares subscribed for by the subscribers to the memorandum of association. [It was noted that the subscribers had waived their rights to share certificates.][3] IT WAS RESOLVED that the names of the subscribers be entered in the register of members in respect of such shares.

10. There were produced to and considered by the meeting the following transfers of shares [with supporting certificates]:
Transferor: *John Doe* Transferee: *James Etheridge* No. of shares: *1*
Transferor: *Joy Stag* Transferee: *Peggy Flanagan* No. of shares: *1*

11. IT WAS RESOLVED that:
a. subject to their being represented duly stamped, such transfers be approved;
b. the names of the transferees be entered in the register of members in respect of the shares transferred to them; and
c. the Secretary be instructed to prepare share certificates in respect of the shares transferred and to deliver them to the transferees.

12. The Secretary was instructed to arrange for a nameplate to be ordered and affixed outside the registered office.

13. The Secretary was instructed to file Form 225 (accounting reference date) with the registrar of companies.[4]

14. IT WAS RESOLVED that the Company should trade under the name *Take Note* .
The Secretary was instructed to ensure compliance with the statutory disclosure requirements in the Business Names Act 1985.

15. The payment of the fees incurred in respect of the formation of the company was approved.

16. The Secretary was instructed to register the company with HM Customs & Excise for the purposes of VAT and to supply particulars to the Inland Revenue for tax purposes.

17. There being no other business the meeting ended.

Chairman: *J. Etheridge*

_____ LIMITED

MINUTES of a Meeting of the Board of Directors held at _____
_____ on _____ at _____ a.m./p.m.

PRESENT:

_____ (in the chair)

_____

_____

_____

IN ATTENDANCE:

_____

_____

_____

The Chairman confirmed that notice of the meeting had been given to all the directors of the Company and that a quorum of the board of directors was present at the meeting.

_____ declared his/their interest(s) in the following contract(s) which were to be discussed at the meeting in accordance with section 317 Companies Act 1985:[1] _____
_____

IT WAS RESOLVED THAT

_____

_____

_____

_____

There being no further business the meeting then ended.

Chairman: _____

[1]_A director is under a duty to declare any interest he may have, whether direct or indirect in a contract or proposed contract with the company at the first meeting at which the question of entering into the contract is considered. If he becomes interested subsequently he must declare his interest at the next board meeting._

Form B05

Law Pack Publishing **LIMITED**

MINUTES of a Meeting of the Board of Directors held at _____
2 James Road, London, SE1 on _Mon 2nd Sept 1999_ at _10.00_ a.m./~~p.m.~~

PRESENT:

James Etheridge (in the chair)

Peggy Flanagan

Russell Coles

IN ATTENDANCE:

Caroline Dore

The Chairman confirmed that notice of the meeting had been given to all the directors of the Company and that a quorum of the board of directors was present at the meeting.

James Etheridge declared his/their interest(s) in the following contract(s) which were to be discussed at the meeting in accordance with section 317 Companies Act 1985:[1]
supply of paper from XYZ Paper, P/O 1234567

IT WAS RESOLVED THAT

Russell Coles shall cease to be secretary of the Company with

effect from 30th September 1999

There being no further business the meeting then ended.

Chairman: _J. Etheridge_

Section C
Board Resolutions

What you'll find in this section:

⟹ Board resolutions for:
- Appointment and removal of officers
- Directors
- Shares
- Constitution

The forms in this section are designed to be used as written resolutions without holding a board meeting (although the text of the resolutions themselves may be inserted into the minutes of a board meeting, as described in Section B). In order to avoid a meeting it is necessary that

- the articles of association allow board resolutions which are signed by the director, see regulation 93 of Table A in Appendix 2.
- the resolution is signed by all the directors entitled to receive notice of a meeting of directors
- the resolution is dated with the date on which it is signed by the last of the directors to sign and is then placed in the company's Minute Book.

If the above conditions are not satisfied, it will be necessary to hold a meeting: see Section B.

Although written resolutions must be signed by every director, they may sign separate copies and the resolutions will then be effective when the last one signs and sends it back to the secretary; a fax may be sent, but the original must also be sent afterwards.

Section contents

Appointment and removal of officers

C01   Appointment of director—Resolves to appoint a director.

C02   Proposal to remove director—Resolves to hold an extraordinary general meeting to propose removing a director.

C03   Appointment of chairman—Resolves to appoint a chairman.

C04   Removal of chairman—Resolves to remove existing chairman.

C05   Appointment of secretary—Resolves to appoint a secretary.

C06   Removal of secretary—Resolves to remove existing secretary.

C07   Appointment of auditors—Resolves to appoint auditors.

C08   Proposal to remove auditors—Resolves to hold an extraordinary general meeting to propose removing auditors.

C09   Notice to auditors of proposed removal—Notifies auditors of an EGM to propose their removal

C10   Appointment of bankers—Resolves to appoint bankers.

Directors

C11   Approval of alternate director—Resolves to approve an alternate director.

C12   Proposal of variation of maximum number of directors—Resolves to hold an extraordinary general meeting to propose limiting the number of directors the company may have.

C13   Proposal of compensation payment—Resolves to hold an extraordinary general meeting to propose giving compensation payment to a resigning board member.

C14   Approval of directors' report and accounts—Resolves to approve the directors' report and annual accounts.

C15   Approval of director's service contract—Resolves to approve a director's service contract with the company for less than five years.

C16   Proposal of approval of director's service contract of more than five years' duration—Resolves to hold an extraordinary general meeting to propose signing a director's service contract of more than five years.

C17   Proposal of director's remuneration—Resolves to hold an extraordinary general meeting to propose paying a director a designated amount.

C18   Proposal to allow director to vote on contracts where there is a personal interest—Resolves to hold an extraordinary general meeting to propose approving of a director voting on contracts with a company of which he is a director or shareholder.

C19   Proposal that members ratify acts of directors beyond the powers delegated to them—Resolves to hold an extraordinary general meeting to propose ratifying acts of the board of directors which were beyond the powers delegated to them.

Shares

C20   Proposal of bonus issue—Resolves to hold an extraordinary general meeting to propose issuing shares by way of a bonus.

C21   Proposal of increase in share capital—Resolves to hold an extraordinary general meeting to propose increasing share capital.

C22   Proposal of reduction in share capital—Resolves to hold an extraordinary general meeting to propose reducing share capital by reducing the nominal amount of each of the issued and unissued shares.

C23   Allotment of shares—Resolves to allot shares to an applicant.

C24   Proposal of dividend—Resolves to hold an extraordinary general meeting to propose paying a dividend to shareholders.

C25   Proposal of purchase of own shares—Resolves to hold an extraordinary general meeting to propose the company's purchase of its own shares from a shareholder.

C26   Proposal of purchase of own shares from capital—Resolves to hold an extraordinary general meeting to propose the company's purchase of its own shares funded from its capital.

C27   Approval and registration of transfer of shares—Approves the transfer of shares from a shareholder to someone else and resolves to register those shares in that person's name.

C28   Proposal that directors be given authority to make a specific allotment of shares for a specified purpose—Resolves to hold an extraordinary general meeting to propose granting directors the authority to make a specific allotment of shares for a specified purpose.

C29   Proposal that directors be given authority to allot shares generally—Resolves to hold an extraordinary general meeting to propose granting directors a general authority to allot shares for a period of up to five years or, if the relevant elective resolution is in place (see Form E20), for an indefinite period.

C30   Proposal of revocation of directors' authority to allot—Resolves to hold an extraordinary general meeting to propose taking away authority previously given to the directors to allot shares.

C31   Proposal of removal of statutory pre-emption rights—Resolves to hold an extraordinary general meeting to propose the removal of the statutory rights of existing shareholders to be offered any shares which are to be allotted before they are allotted to anyone else.

Constitution

C32   Proposal of alteration of articles—Resolves to hold an extraordinary general meeting to propose changing the articles of association.

C33   Proposal of alteration of objects—Resolves to hold an extraordinary general meeting to propose changing the objects of the company as they are set out in the memorandum of association.

C34   Proposal of alteration of articles - no retirement by rotation—Resolves to hold an EGM to propose changing the articles so that directors do not have to retire by rotation.

C35   Proposal of alteration of articles - removal of chairman's casting vote— Resolves to hold an EGM to propose changing the articles so that the chairman shall not have a casting vote.

C36   Proposal of alteration of articles - director voting where personal interest—Resolves to hold an EGM to propose changing the articles so that the chairman shall not have a casting vote.

C37   Proposal of alteration of articles - refusal to register transfer of shares— Resolves to hold an EGM to change the articles so that directors do not have register the transfer of a share.

C38   Proposal of alteration of articles - exclusion of statutory pre-emption rights— Resolves to hold an EGM to change the articles so that the statutory rights of existing shareholders to be offered any shares which are to be allotted before they are allotted to anyone else are excluded.

C39   Proposal of alteration of articles - quorum for general meeting—Resolves to hold an EGM to change the articles so that if a quorum is not present at a general meeting the meeting be adjourned.

C40   Proposal of alteration of articles - number of directors—Resolves to hold an EGM to change the articles so that number of directors may be varied.

C41   Proposal of alteration of articles - alternate directors—Resolves to hold an EGM to propose changing the articles so that directors may specify that a proportion of their remuneration is paid to their alternate.

C42   Proposal of alteration of articles - weighted voting rights—Resolves to hold an EGM to change the articles so that voting rights of directors are weighted according to number of shares held, in order to prevent the directors from being removed from office.

C43   Proposal of alteration of articles - authority to allot shares—Resolves to hold an EGM to change the articles so that directors have authority to allot shares.

C44   Proposal of adoption of new articles—Resolves to hold an EGM to propose adopting new articles of association.

C45   Proposal of name change—Resolves to hold an extraordinary general meeting to propose changing the name of the company.

C46   Adoption of trading name—Resolves to adopt a trading name.

C47   Proposal of elective resolutions—Resolves to hold an extraordinary general meeting to propose the removal of certain restrictions in the company's articles of association. Cross out any provisions that do not apply.

C48   Proposal that company re-register as a Public Limited Company—Resolves to hold an extraordinary general meeting to propose re-registering as a public limited company.

C49   Change address of registered office—Resolves to change the address of the registered office.

C50   Adoption of company seal—Resolves to adopt a company seal.

Financial

C51   Change of accounting reference date—Resolves to change the date on which the company's financial year ends.

C52   Proposal of voluntary liquidation where company insolvent—Resolves to hold an extraordinary general meeting to propose beginning to wind up because the company is insolvent and cannot pay its debts.

C53   Proposal of voluntary liquidation where company solvent—Resolves to hold an extraordinary general meeting to propose the winding up of the company.

C54   Application for an administration order—Resolves to apply for an administrator to be appointed to run the company while it is unable to pay its debts.

C55   Approval of auditors' remuneration for audit—Resolves to pay the auditors a fee for auditing the annual financial records.

C56   Approval of auditors' remuneration for services and advice—Resolves to pay the company's auditors a fee for their services and advice.

C57   Registration for VAT—Resolves to register for value added tax. Registration is obligatory if value of taxable supplies in the past 12 months or less has exceeded £49,000.

C58   Issue of debenture—Resolves to give the directors authority to issue a document stating the terms of a loan.

C59   Proposal of approval of substantial property transaction—Resolves to hold an extraordinary general meeting to approve a substantial property transaction involving a director of the company.

Company Number: _____

THE COMPANIES ACT 1985
PRIVATE COMPANY LIMITED BY SHARES
WRITTEN RESOLUTION OF THE BOARD OF DIRECTORS

_____ **LIMITED**

Pursuant to the articles of association of the company the undersigned, being all the directors of the company, hereby resolve:

THAT _____ , having indicated his/her willingness to act, be appointed as a director of the Company with effect from _____ [1] .

Directors' signatures: Date of each signature:

_____   _____

_____   _____

_____   _____

[1] *Table A, article 79 provides that this appointment only stands until the company's next AGM.*

Form C01

Company Number: _____

THE COMPANIES ACT 1985
PRIVATE COMPANY LIMITED BY SHARES
WRITTEN RESOLUTION OF THE BOARD OF DIRECTORS

_____ LIMITED

Pursuant to the articles of association of the company, the undersigned, being all the directors of the company, hereby resolve:

THAT an extraordinary general meeting be convened to propose the removal of _____
as director with effect from _____ .[1]

Directors' signatures: Date of each signature:

_____   _____

_____   _____

_____   _____

[1] *Must give special notice of this resolution i.e. must leave formal notice at the registered office at least 28 days before the general meeting. The company must inform the director concerned (see Forms D09-D11). The written resolution procedure cannot be used.*

Company Number: _____

THE COMPANIES ACT 1985
PRIVATE COMPANY LIMITED BY SHARES
WRITTEN RESOLUTION OF THE BOARD OF DIRECTORS

_____ LIMITED

Pursuant to the articles of association of the company the undersigned, being all the directors of the company, hereby resolve:

THAT _____ , be appointed as chairman of the Company with effect from _____.

Directors' signatures: Date of each signature:

_____   _____

_____   _____

_____   _____

Company Number: _____

THE COMPANIES ACT 1985
PRIVATE COMPANY LIMITED BY SHARES
WRITTEN RESOLUTION OF THE BOARD OF DIRECTORS

_____ LIMITED

Pursuant to the articles of association of the company the undersigned, being all the directors of the company, hereby resolve:

THAT _____ , shall cease to be chairman of the Company with effect from _____ .

Directors' signatures: Date of each signature:

_____   _____

_____   _____

_____   _____

Company Number: _____

THE COMPANIES ACT 1985
PRIVATE COMPANY LIMITED BY SHARES
WRITTEN RESOLUTION OF THE BOARD OF DIRECTORS

_____ **LIMITED**

Pursuant to the articles of association of the company the undersigned, being all the directors of the company, hereby resolve:

THAT _____ , having indicated his/her willingness to act, be appointed as secretary of the Company with effect from _____.[1]

Directors' signatures: Date of each signature:

_____   _____

_____   _____

_____   _____

[1] *File Companies House form 288a.*

Form C05

Company Number: _____

THE COMPANIES ACT 1985
PRIVATE COMPANY LIMITED BY SHARES
WRITTEN RESOLUTION OF THE BOARD OF DIRECTORS

_____ LIMITED

Pursuant to the articles of association of the company the undersigned, being all the directors of the company, hereby resolve:

THAT _____ , shall cease to be secretary of the Company with effect from _____.[1]

Directors' signatures: Date of each signature:

_____   _____

_____   _____

_____   _____

[1]*File Companies House form 288b .*

Company Number: _____

THE COMPANIES ACT 1985
PRIVATE COMPANY LIMITED BY SHARES
WRITTEN RESOLUTION OF THE BOARD OF DIRECTORS

_____ LIMITED

Pursuant to the articles of association of the company the undersigned, being all the directors of the company, hereby resolve:

THAT _____

of _____ be the auditors

of the Company with effect from _____

at a fee to be agreed.[1]

Directors' signatures: Date of each signature:

_____   _____

_____   _____

_____   _____

[1]*Generally, the directors may appoint only the first auditors of the company who may hold office until the conclusion of the first general meeting of the company. The auditors must then be re-appointed or an alternative firm appointed by a resolution of the shareholders on an annual basis. The directors may also, however, fill any casual vacancy in the office of auditor. It should be noted that an elective resolution may be passed which removes the requirement for auditors to be re-appointed annually (see Forms C47 and E23).*

Company Number: _____

THE COMPANIES ACT 1985
PRIVATE COMPANY LIMITED BY SHARES
WRITTEN RESOLUTION OF THE BOARD OF DIRECTORS

_____ LIMITED

Pursuant to the articles of association of the company the undersigned, being all the directors of the company, hereby resolve:

THAT an extraordinary general meeting be held at _____ _____ on _____ at _____ am/pm to propose the removal of Messrs _____ as auditors of the Company with effect from _____.[1]

Directors' signatures: Date of each signature:

_____   _____

_____   _____

_____   _____

[1]This resolution is to be used where the auditors are to be removed before their term of office has expired.
[2]Must give special notice of this resolution, see Form D13. This cannot be done by the written resolution procedure. Notice must be given to the auditors, see Form C09.

_____ LIMITED

Dear Sirs

This letter[1] is to give you formal notice that the enclosed special notice of a resolution that you be removed as the company's auditors has been received by the company in accordance with section 391A Companies Act 1985. The directors have resolved to convene an Extraordinary General Meeting for the purpose of considering, and if thought fit, passing this resolution.

In accordance with section 391A of the Companies Act 1985 you are entitled to make representations in writing in respect of this resolution and to have them circulated to all the members of the company. If you wish to make any representations to the company, please send them, in writing, by _____ .[2]

Yours faithfully

_____

Director/Secretary

[1]Send as soon as special notice is received. Enclose a copy of the special notice. See Form D14 for Notice concerning this meeting.
[2]Insert date on which Notice of EGM is to be sent to shareholders.

Company Number: _____

THE COMPANIES ACT 1985
PRIVATE COMPANY LIMITED BY SHARES
WRITTEN RESOLUTION OF THE BOARD OF DIRECTORS

_____ LIMITED

Pursuant to the articles of association of the company the undersigned, being all the directors of the company, hereby resolve:

THAT _____

of _____

be appointed as the bankers of the Company, that the resolutions contained in the Bank's formal mandate annexed hereto be approved and deemed to be set out in this resolution in extenso and that the signatories named therein be authorised to sign the same as appropriate.[1]

Directors' signatures: Date of each signature:

_____   _____

_____   _____

_____   _____

[1]*Attach copy of bank's formal mandate*

Company Number: _____

THE COMPANIES ACT 1985
PRIVATE COMPANY LIMITED BY SHARES
WRITTEN RESOLUTION OF THE BOARD OF DIRECTORS

_____ LIMITED

Pursuant to the articles of association of the company the undersigned, being all the directors of the company, hereby resolve:

THAT the appointment of _____ , having indicated his/her willingness to act, as alternate director for _____ be approved.[1]

Directors' signatures: Date of each signature:

_____   _____

_____   _____

_____   _____

[1] File Companies House form 288a in respect of appointment of alternate director.

Company Number: _____

THE COMPANIES ACT 1985
PRIVATE COMPANY LIMITED BY SHARES
WRITTEN RESOLUTION OF THE BOARD OF DIRECTORS

_____ LIMITED

Pursuant to the articles of association of the company the undersigned, being all the directors of the company, hereby resolve:

THAT an extraordinary general meeting be convened to propose that the maximum number of directors be fixed at _____ and that the company's articles of association be amended accordingly.

Directors' signatures: Date of each signature:

_____   _____

_____   _____

_____   _____

Company Number: _____

THE COMPANIES ACT 1985
PRIVATE COMPANY LIMITED BY SHARES
WRITTEN RESOLUTION OF THE BOARD OF DIRECTORS

_____ LIMITED

Pursuant to the articles of association of the company the undersigned, being all the directors of the company, hereby resolve:

THAT an extraordinary general meeting be convened to propose that compensation of _____

be paid to _____

on his resignation from the Board.

Directors' signatures: Date of each signature:

_____   _____

_____   _____

_____   _____

Company Number: _____

THE COMPANIES ACT 1985
PRIVATE COMPANY LIMITED BY SHARES
WRITTEN RESOLUTION OF THE BOARD OF DIRECTORS

_____ LIMITED

Pursuant to the articles of association of the company the undersigned, being all the directors of the company, hereby resolve:

THAT the directors' report and accounts for the year ended _____ have been prepared in accordance with the Companies Act 1985 and are hereby approved, and _____ be authorised to sign the report and the balance sheet on behalf of the company.

Directors' signatures: Date of each signature:

_____   _____

_____   _____

_____   _____

Company Number: _____

THE COMPANIES ACT 1985
PRIVATE COMPANY LIMITED BY SHARES
WRITTEN RESOLUTION OF THE BOARD OF DIRECTORS

_____ LIMITED

Pursuant to the articles of association of the company, the undersigned, being all the directors of the company and having formally declared their interests in the matter in accordance with section 317 of the Companies Act 1985 hereby resolve to approve the terms of the the proposed service contract between the Company and _____

_____

in the terms set out in the copy annexed hereto.[1]

Directors' signatures: Date of each signature:

_____   _____

_____   _____

_____   _____

[1]If service contracts are for a fixed term over five years, the members must approve the terms by an ordinary resolution in a general meeting.

Company Number: _____

THE COMPANIES ACT 1985
PRIVATE COMPANY LIMITED BY SHARES
WRITTEN RESOLUTION OF THE BOARD OF DIRECTORS

_____ LIMITED

Pursuant to the articles of association of the company and s.319 of the Companies Act 1985 and the directors having formally declared their interests in the matter in accordance with section 317 of the Companies Act 1985, the undersigned, being all directors of the company hereby resolve:

THAT an extraordinary general meeting be convened to propose that

_____

be awarded a service contract in excess of five years on the terms annexed hereto and hereby approved by the directors.

Directors' signatures: Date of each signature:

_____   _____

_____   _____

_____   _____

Company Number: _____

THE COMPANIES ACT 1985
PRIVATE COMPANY LIMITED BY SHARES
WRITTEN RESOLUTION OF THE BOARD OF DIRECTORS

_____ LIMITED

Pursuant to the articles of association of the company, the undersigned, being all the directors of the company, hereby resolve:

THAT an extraordinary general meeting be convened to propose that the payment of £ _____

be paid to _____

as remuneration on a _____ basis.

Directors' signatures: Date of each signature:

_____   _____

_____   _____

_____   _____

Company Number: _____

THE COMPANIES ACT 1985
PRIVATE COMPANY LIMITED BY SHARES
WRITTEN RESOLUTION OF THE BOARD OF DIRECTORS

_____ LIMITED

Pursuant to the articles of association of the company, the undersigned, being all the directors of the company, hereby resolve:

THAT an extraordinary general meeting be convened to propose that in accordance with Table A, article 96 (which is incorporated in the articles of association of the company by virtue of article _____ of those articles), _____ who is a director of this company, may vote on contracts between this company and _____ notwithstanding that he has declared his interest as a director/shareholder of _____ .

Directors' signatures: Date of each signature:

_____   _____

_____   _____

_____   _____

Company Number: _____

THE COMPANIES ACT 1985
PRIVATE COMPANY LIMITED BY SHARES
WRITTEN RESOLUTION OF THE BOARD OF DIRECTORS

_____ LIMITED

Pursuant to the articles of association of the company, the undersigned, being all the directors of the company, hereby resolve:

THAT an extraordinary general meeting be convened to propose that all acts of the directors done prior to the date of this resolution be confirmed and ratified notwithstanding any matter that might otherwise cause their validity to be in doubt.[1]

Directors' signatures: Date of each signature:

_____   _____

_____   _____

_____   _____

[1]Where the board of directors act beyond the powers delegated to them by the company's articles this may be ratified by an ordinary resolution of the members of the type proposed here. If the directors act beyond the powers of the company as set out in the objects clause in its memorandum of association, legal advice should be sought.

Company Number: _____

THE COMPANIES ACT 1985
PRIVATE COMPANY LIMITED BY SHARES
WRITTEN RESOLUTION OF THE BOARD OF DIRECTORS

_____ LIMITED

Pursuant to the articles of association of the company, the undersigned, being all the directors of the company, hereby resolve:

THAT an extraordinary general meeting be convened to approve the capitalisation of £_____
of the company's profits by way of the issue of _____
share(s) for every _____ share(s) already held.

Directors' signatures: Date of each signature:

_____   _____

_____   _____

_____   _____

Company Number: _____

THE COMPANIES ACT 1985
PRIVATE COMPANY LIMITED BY SHARES
WRITTEN RESOLUTION OF THE BOARD OF DIRECTORS

_____ LIMITED

Pursuant to the articles of association of the company, the undersigned, being all the directors of the company, hereby resolve:

THAT an extraordinary general meeting be convened to propose that the authorised share capital of the Company be increased by £ _____ [1] from £ _____ divided into _____ ordinary shares of _____ each to £ _____ divided into _____ ordinary shares of _____ each.

Directors' signatures: Date of each signature:

_____   _____

_____   _____

_____   _____

[1] The authorised share capital can only be increased if the Articles allow it. The notice of the extraordinary general meeting must state the amount of the proposed increase. The increase must be notified to Companies House on Companies House form 123.

Company Number: _____

THE COMPANIES ACT 1985
PRIVATE COMPANY LIMITED BY SHARES
WRITTEN RESOLUTION OF THE BOARD OF DIRECTORS

_____ LIMITED

Pursuant to the articles of association of the company, the undersigned, being all the directors of the company, hereby resolve:

THAT in accordance with s.135 of the Companies act 1985 an extraordinary general meeting be convened to propose to reduce the authorised share capital of the company from £ _____ to £ _____ by cancelling paid up capital to the extent of _____ on each of the shares of _____ each in the capital of the company and reducing the nominal amount of each of the issued and unissued shares from _____ to _____ accordingly.[1]

Directors' signatures: Date of each signature:

_____   _____

_____   _____

_____   _____

[1]_The rules governing a company's ability to reduce its share capital are complex and the procedure involves obtaining the consent of the court. This resolution should therefore not be used without first taking the advice of the company's solicitors._

Company Number: _____

THE COMPANIES ACT 1985
PRIVATE COMPANY LIMITED BY SHARES
WRITTEN RESOLUTION OF THE BOARD OF DIRECTORS

_____ LIMITED

Pursuant to the articles of association of the company, the undersigned, being all the directors of the company, hereby resolve THAT the application from _____ annexed hereto for the allotment to him/her of _____ shares of _____each for an aggregate consideration of £ _____ / in consideration of _____ be accepted and _____ shares of £ _____ each in the capital of the Company be allotted to _____ on the terms of his/her application.[1]

Directors' signatures: Date of each signature:

_____   _____

_____   _____

_____   _____

[1]*Check the articles - directors can only allot shares if they have the authority to do so. If they do not have the authority, the members can give it to them by an ordinary resolution (see Forms E06 and E07). Update the register of members. File Companies House form 88(2). Prepare a share certificate.*

Company Number: _____

THE COMPANIES ACT 1985
PRIVATE COMPANY LIMITED BY SHARES
WRITTEN RESOLUTION OF THE BOARD OF DIRECTORS

_____ LIMITED

Pursuant to the articles of association of the company, the undersigned, being all the directors of the company, hereby resolve:

THAT an extraordinary general meeting be convened to declare a dividend of _____ p per share in respect of the year ended _____ on the ordinary shares of _____ each in the capital of the Company payable on _____ to the holders of ordinary shares registered at the close of business on

_____ .

Directors' signatures: Date of each signature:

_____   _____

_____   _____

_____   _____

Company Number: _____

THE COMPANIES ACT 1985
PRIVATE COMPANY LIMITED BY SHARES
WRITTEN RESOLUTION OF THE BOARD OF DIRECTORS

_____ LIMITED

Pursuant to the articles of association of the company, the undersigned, being all the directors of the company, hereby resolve:

THAT in accordance with section 162 of the Companies Act 1985 an extraordinary general meeting be convened to propose that the Company purchase _____
of its own shares from _____
on the terms of the contract attached to this resolution, the payment for such shares to be made from the Company's distributable profits / the proceeds of a fresh issue of shares.[2]

Directors' signatures: Date of each signature:

_____   _____

_____   _____

_____   _____

[1]A company is allowed to purchase its own shares only in limited circumstances and the directors should not pass this resolution without first seeking the advice of the company's auditors.
[2]Delete as appropriate. The articles must allow a buy-back. Table A, article 35 does.

Form C25

Company Number: _____

THE COMPANIES ACT 1985
PRIVATE COMPANY LIMITED BY SHARES
WRITTEN RESOLUTION OF THE BOARD OF DIRECTORS

_____ LIMITED

Pursuant to the articles of association of the company, the undersigned, being all the directors of the company, hereby resolve:

THAT in accordance with section 171 of the Companies Act 1985 an extraordinary general meeting be convened to propose that the Company purchase its own shares, on terms produced to this meeting, and that payment for the purchase shall be made from the capital[1] of the Company.[2]

Directors' signatures: Date of each signature:

_____   _____

_____   _____

_____   _____

[1]A company may only purchase its own shares out of capital (i.e. otherwise than from distributable profits or the proceeds of a fresh issue of shares) as a last resort. The rules governing such a purchase and the tax treatment of money paid to shareholders are complex and this resolution should not be used without first seeking the advice of the company's auditors and solicitors.
[2]The articles must allow this. Table A, article 35 does. The directors must make a statutory declaration of solvency supported by a report given by the company's auditors within a week of the resolution passed at the EGM. A notice to creditors must appear in the London Gazette (tel. 0171 394 4580) and a national newspaper within a week of the members' resolution.

Company Number: _____

THE COMPANIES ACT 1985
PRIVATE COMPANY LIMITED BY SHARES
WRITTEN RESOLUTION OF THE BOARD OF DIRECTORS

_____ LIMITED

Pursuant to the articles of association of the company, the undersigned, being all the directors of the company, hereby resolve:

THAT in accordance with the Company's Articles of Association and subject to its being represented duly stamped the directors approve the transfer of _____ shares of _____ each from

_____

to _____
on _____,
THAT the name of _____
be entered in the register of members in respect of the shares transferred to him/her and THAT the Secretary be instructed to prepare a share certificate in respect of the shares transferred and to deliver it to

_____ .[1]

Directors' signatures: Date of each signature:

_____   _____

_____   _____

_____   _____

[1]Check the articles - they may have a restriction on the transfer of shares. Table A places no restrictions on transfers of fully-paid shares. They may also allow the directors to refuse to register a transfer, although again Table A does not allow them to refuse to register the transfer of fully-paid shares.

Company Number: _____

THE COMPANIES ACT 1985
PRIVATE COMPANY LIMITED BY SHARES
WRITTEN RESOLUTION OF THE BOARD OF DIRECTORS

_____ LIMITED

Pursuant to the articles of association of the company, the undersigned, being all the directors of the company, hereby resolve:

THAT an extraordinary general meeting be convened to propose that the directors be given authority pursuant to section 80 of the Companies Act 1985 to make a specific allotment of up to _____ shares in the capital of the company for the purposes of _____ _____ .

Directors' signatures: Date of each signature:

_____   _____

_____   _____

_____   _____

Company Number: _____

THE COMPANIES ACT 1985
PRIVATE COMPANY LIMITED BY SHARES
WRITTEN RESOLUTION OF THE BOARD OF DIRECTORS

_____ LIMITED

Pursuant to the articles of association of the company, the undersigned, being all the directors of the company, hereby resolve:

THAT an extraordinary general meeting be convened to propose that the directors be given general and unconditional authority pursuant to section 80 of the Companies Act 1985 to allot up to _____ shares of _____ each in the capital of the company during the period of _____months/years from the granting of such authority.[1]

Directors' signatures: Date of each signature:

_____   _____

_____   _____

_____   _____

[1]Unless the members pass an elective resolution (see Form E25), the authority may only be given for up to a maximum period of 5 years from the date of the passing of the members' resolution.

Company Number: _____

THE COMPANIES ACT 1985
PRIVATE COMPANY LIMITED BY SHARES
WRITTEN RESOLUTION OF THE BOARD OF DIRECTORS

_____ LIMITED

Pursuant to the articles of association of the company, the undersigned, being all the directors of the company, hereby resolve:

THAT an extraordinary general meeting be convened to propose that the members revoke the directors' authority to allot shares pursuant to s.80 of the Companies Act 1985 given in a resolution dated _____ .

Directors' signatures: Date of each signature:

_____   _____

_____   _____

_____   _____

Company Number: _____

THE COMPANIES ACT 1985
PRIVATE COMPANY LIMITED BY SHARES
WRITTEN RESOLUTION OF THE BOARD OF DIRECTORS

_____ LIMITED

Pursuant to the articles of association of the company, the undersigned, being all the directors of the company, hereby resolve:

THAT an extraordinary general meeting be convened to propose that the members authorise the directors to allot shares pursuant to the authority conferred on them under section 80 of the Companies Act 1985 by a resolution passed on _____
as if section 89(1) of that Act did not apply to the allotment.

Directors' signatures: Date of each signature:

_____   _____

_____   _____

_____   _____

Company Number: _____

THE COMPANIES ACT 1985
PRIVATE COMPANY LIMITED BY SHARES
WRITTEN RESOLUTION OF THE BOARD OF DIRECTORS

_____ LIMITED

Pursuant to the articles of association of the company, the undersigned, being all the directors of the company, hereby resolve:

THAT an extraordinary general meeting be convened to authorise the alteration of the articles as set out below

(1) By deletion of articles _____
    and _____
    and altering the subsequent numbering accordingly.

(2) By the addition of the new articles as set out in the attached
    document to be numbered _____
    and _____ .

Directors' signatures: Date of each signature:

_____   _____

_____   _____

_____   _____

Company Number: _____

THE COMPANIES ACT 1985
PRIVATE COMPANY LIMITED BY SHARES
WRITTEN RESOLUTION OF THE BOARD OF DIRECTORS

_____ **LIMITED**

Pursuant to the articles of association of the company, the undersigned, being all the directors of the company, hereby resolve:

THAT an extraordinary general meeting be convened to authorise the alteration of the objects of the Company contained in the Company's memorandum of association in accordance with the document annexed hereto.

Directors' signatures: Date of each signature:

_____   _____

_____   _____

_____   _____

Company Number: _____

THE COMPANIES ACT 1985
PRIVATE COMPANY LIMITED BY SHARES
WRITTEN RESOLUTION OF THE BOARD OF DIRECTORS

_____ LIMITED

Pursuant to the articles of association of the company, the undersigned, being all the directors of the company, hereby resolve:

THAT an extraordinary general meeting be convened to authorise the alteration of the articles by the insertion of the wording set out below as new article no._____ and the renumbering of the subsequent articles accordingly/in substitution for the existing article no._____.[1]

The Directors shall not be required to retire by rotation and regulations 73 to 80 (inclusive) in Table A shall not apply to the Company.

Directors' signatures: Date of each signature:

_____   _____

_____   _____

_____   _____

[1]*Delete as appropriate. NB this form is for use only where the Table A regulations referred to in the resolution are presently incorporated in the company's articles.*

Company Number: _____

THE COMPANIES ACT 1985
PRIVATE COMPANY LIMITED BY SHARES
WRITTEN RESOLUTION OF THE BOARD OF DIRECTORS

_____ LIMITED

Pursuant to the articles of association of the company, the undersigned, being all the directors of the company, hereby resolve:

THAT an extraordinary general meeting be convened to authorise the alteration of the articles by the insertion of the wording set out below as new article no.____ and the renumbering of the subsequent articles accordingly/in substitution for the existing article no.____.[1]

The Chairman shall not have a casting vote and regulation 50 in Table A shall not apply to the company.

Directors' signatures: Date of each signature:

_____   _____

_____   _____

_____   _____

[1]_Delete as appropriate. NB this form is for use only where the Table A regulations referred to in the resolution are presently incorporated in the company's articles._

Company Number: _____

THE COMPANIES ACT 1985
PRIVATE COMPANY LIMITED BY SHARES
WRITTEN RESOLUTION OF THE BOARD OF DIRECTORS

_____ **LIMITED**

Pursuant to the articles of association of the company, the undersigned, being all the directors of the company, hereby resolve:

THAT an extraordinary general meeting be convened to authorise the alteration of the articles by the insertion of the wording set out below as new article no.____ and the renumbering of the subsequent articles accordingly/in substitution for the existing article no.____.[1]

(a) A Director may vote at any meeting of the Directors or of any Committee of the Directors on any resolution notwithstanding that it in any way con-cerns or relates to a matter in which he has, directly or indirectly, any kind of interest whatsoever and if he shall vote on any such resolution as afore-said his vote shall be counted and in relation to any such resolution as aforesaid he shall (whether or not he shall vote on the same) be taken into account in calculating the quorum present at the meeting.

(b) Regulations 94 to 97 (inclusive) in Table A shall not apply to the company.

Directors' signatures: Date of each signature:

_____   _____

_____   _____

_____   _____

[1]*Delete as appropriate. NB this form is for use only where the Table A regulations referred to in the resolution are presently incorporated in the company's articles.*

Company Number: _____

THE COMPANIES ACT 1985
PRIVATE COMPANY LIMITED BY SHARES
WRITTEN RESOLUTION OF THE BOARD OF DIRECTORS

_____ LIMITED

Pursuant to the articles of association of the company, the undersigned, being all the directors of the company, hereby resolve:

THAT an extraordinary general meeting be convened to authorise the alteration of the articles by the insertion of the wording set out below as new article no.____ and the renumbering of the subsequent articles accordingly/in substitution for the existing article no.____.[1]

> The Directors may, in their absolute discretion and without assigning any reason, decline to register the transfer of a share, whether or not it is a fully paid share and regulation 24 in Table A shall not apply to the Company.

Directors' signatures: Date of each signature:

_____   _____

_____   _____

_____   _____

Company Number: _____

THE COMPANIES ACT 1985
PRIVATE COMPANY LIMITED BY SHARES
WRITTEN RESOLUTION OF THE BOARD OF DIRECTORS

_____ LIMITED

Pursuant to the articles of association of the company, the undersigned, being all the directors of the company, hereby resolve:

THAT an extraordinary general meeting be convened to authorise the alteration of the articles by the insertion of the wording set out below as new article no.____ and the renumbering of the subsequent articles accordingly/in substitution for the existing article no.____.[1]

In accordance with section 91(1) of the Companies Act 1985, sections 89(1) and 90(1) to (6) (inclusive) shall not apply to the company.

Directors' signatures: Date of each signature:

_____   _____

_____   _____

_____   _____

[1]Delete as appropriate. NB this form is for use only where the Table A regulations referred to in the resolution are presently incorporated in the company's articles.

Company Number: _____

THE COMPANIES ACT 1985
PRIVATE COMPANY LIMITED BY SHARES
WRITTEN RESOLUTION OF THE BOARD OF DIRECTORS

_____ LIMITED

Pursuant to the articles of association of the company, the undersigned, being all the directors of the company, hereby resolve:

THAT an extraordinary general meeting be convened to authorise the alteration of the articles by the insertion of the wording set out below as new article no.___ and the renumbering of the subsequent articles accordingly/in substitution for the existing article no.____.[1]

(a) If a quorum is not present within half an hour from the time appointed for a general meeting the general meeting shall stand adjourned to the same day in the next week at the same time and place or to such other day and at such other time and place as the directors may determine and if at the adjourned general meeting a quorum is not present within half an hour from the time appointed such adjourned general meeting shall be dissolved.

(b) Regulation 41 in Table A shall not apply to the company.

Directors' signatures: Date of each signature:

_____   _____

_____   _____

_____   _____

[1]Delete as appropriate. NB this form is for use only where the Table A regulations referred to in the resolution are presently incorporated in the company's articles.

Company Number: _____

THE COMPANIES ACT 1985
PRIVATE COMPANY LIMITED BY SHARES
WRITTEN RESOLUTION OF THE BOARD OF DIRECTORS

_____ LIMITED

Pursuant to the articles of association of the company, the undersigned, being all the directors of the company, hereby resolve:

THAT an extraordinary general meeting be convened to authorise the alteration of the articles by the insertion of the wording set out below as new article no.____ and the renumbering of the subsequent articles accordingly/in substitution for the existing article no.____.[1]

(a)   Regulation 64 in Table A shall not apply to the company.

(b)   The maximum number and minimum number respectively of the directors may be determined from time to time by ordinary resolution in general meeting of the company. Subject to and in default of any such determination there shall be no maximum number of directors and the minimum number of directors shall be one. Whensoever the minimum number of directors shall be one, a sole director shall have authority to exercise all the powers and discretions expressed by these articles to be vested in the directors generally and regulation 89 in Table A shall be modified accordingly.

Directors' signatures: Date of each signature:

_____   _____

_____   _____

_____   _____

[1]_Delete as appropriate. NB this form is for use only where the Table A regulations referred to in the resolution are presently incorporated in the company's articles._

Company Number: _____

THE COMPANIES ACT 1985
PRIVATE COMPANY LIMITED BY SHARES
WRITTEN RESOLUTION OF THE BOARD OF DIRECTORS

_____ LIMITED

Pursuant to the articles of association of the company, the undersigned, being all the directors of the company, hereby resolve:

THAT an extraordinary general meeting be convened to authorise the alteration of the articles by the insertion of the wording set out below as new article no.____ and the renumbering of the subsequent articles accordingly/in substitution for the existing article no.____.[1]

> An alternate director shall not be entitled to receive any remuneration from the company, save that he may be paid by the company such part (if any) of the remuneration otherwise payable to his appointor as such appointor may by notice in writing to the company form time to time direct and the first sentence of regulation 66 in Table A shall be modified accordingly

Directors' signatures: Date of each signature:

_____   _____

_____   _____

_____   _____

[1]Delete as appropriate. NB this form is for use only where the Table A regulations referred to in the resolution are presently incorporated in the company's articles.

Company Number: _____

THE COMPANIES ACT 1985
PRIVATE COMPANY LIMITED BY SHARES
WRITTEN RESOLUTION OF THE BOARD OF DIRECTORS

_____ LIMITED

Pursuant to the articles of association of the company, the undersigned, being all the directors of the company, hereby resolve:

THAT an extraordinary general meeting be convened to authorise the alteration of the articles by the insertion of the wording set out below as new article no.____ and the renumbering of the subsequent articles accordingly/in substitution for the existing article no.____.[1]

Every director for the time being of the company shall have the following rights:

(a)   if at any general meeting a resolution is proposed to remove him from office, he shall be entitled to demand a poll and on that poll he shall have when voting against such resolution ____[2] votes for each share of which he is the holder; and

(b)   if at any general meeting a poll is duly demanded on a resolution to delete or amend the provisions of this article, he shall be entitled to demand a poll and on that poll he shall have when voting against such resolution ____[3] votes for each share of which he is the holder.

and regulation 54 in Table A shall be modified accordingly.

Directors' signatures: Date of each signature:

_____   _____

_____   _____

_____   _____

[1] *Delete as appropriate. This article will have the effect of preventing the directors (as long as they are also shareholders) from being removed from office.*
[2] *Insert the relevant number which will ensure that each director has more than 50% of the votes in this situation.*
[3] *Insert the relevant number which will ensure that each director has more than 75% of the votes in this situation.*
NB this form is for use only where the Table A regulations referred to in the resolution are presently incorporated in the company's articles.

Company Number: _____

THE COMPANIES ACT 1985
PRIVATE COMPANY LIMITED BY SHARES
WRITTEN RESOLUTION OF THE BOARD OF DIRECTORS

_____ LIMITED

Pursuant to the articles of association of the company, the undersigned, being all the directors of the company, hereby resolve:

THAT an extraordinary general meeting be convened to authorise the alteration of the articles by the insertion of the wording set out below as new article no.____ and the renumbering of the subsequent articles accordingly/in substitution for the existing article no.____.[1]

> The directors are generally and unconditionally authorised for the purposes of s.80 of the Companies Act to exercise any powers of the company to allot and grant rights to subscribe for or convert securities into share of the company up to the amount of the authorised share capital with which the company is incorporated at any time or times during the period of the five years from the date of incorporation and the directors may after that period allot any shares or grant any such rights under this authority in pursuance of an offer or agreement so to do made by the company within that period. The authority hereby given may at any time (subject to s.80 of the Companies Act 1985) be renewed, revoked or varied by ordinary resolution of the company in general meeting.

Directors' signatures: Date of each signature:

_____   _____

_____   _____

_____   _____

[1] Delete as appropriate. NB this form is for use only where the Table A regulations referred to in the resolution are presently incorporated in the company's articles.

Form C43

Company Number: _____

THE COMPANIES ACT 1985
PRIVATE COMPANY LIMITED BY SHARES
WRITTEN RESOLUTION OF THE BOARD OF DIRECTORS

_____ **LIMITED**

Pursuant to the articles of association of the company, the undersigned, being all the directors of the company, hereby resolve:

THAT an extraordinary general meeting be convened to authorise the adoption of new articles of association in the form annexed hereto.

Directors' signatures: Date of each signature:

_____   _____

_____   _____

_____   _____

Company Number: _____

THE COMPANIES ACT 1985
PRIVATE COMPANY LIMITED BY SHARES
WRITTEN RESOLUTION OF THE BOARD OF DIRECTORS

_____ LIMITED

Pursuant to the articles of association of the company, the undersigned, being all the directors of the company, hereby resolve:

THAT an extraordinary general meeting be convened to propose that the name of the company be changed to _____ with effect from _____.[1]

Directors' signatures: Date of each signature:

_____   _____

_____   _____

_____   _____

[1]*Copy of special resolution passed at EGM and amended print of the company's memorandum and articles of association will need to be filed at Companies House.*

Company Number: _____

THE COMPANIES ACT 1985
PRIVATE COMPANY LIMITED BY SHARES
WRITTEN RESOLUTION OF THE BOARD OF DIRECTORS

_____ LIMITED

Pursuant to the articles of association of the company, the undersigned, being all the directors of the company, hereby resolve:

THAT the Company should trade under the name '_____ _____' and that the Secretary be instructed to ensure compliance with the statutory disclosure requirements in the Business Names Act 1985.

Directors' signatures: Date of each signature:

_____   _____

_____   _____

_____   _____

Company Number: _____

THE COMPANIES ACT 1985
PRIVATE COMPANY LIMITED BY SHARES
WRITTEN RESOLUTION OF THE BOARD OF DIRECTORS

_____ LIMITED

Pursuant to the articles of association of the company, the undersigned, being all the directors of the company, hereby resolve:

THAT in accordance with s.379A of the Companies Act 1985, an extraordinary general meeting be convened to propose the introduction of the following elective resolution(s):[1]

(1) That in accordance with s.366A of the Companies Act 1985 the Company hereby elects to dispense with the requirement to hold annual general meetings until this resolution is revoked.[2]

(2) That in accordance with s.252A of the Companies Act 1985 the Company hereby elects to dispense with the requirement of laying accounts and reports before the Company in a general meeting.[3]

(3) That in accordance with s.386A of the Companies Act 1985 the Company hereby elects to dispense with the obligation to appoint auditors annually.

(4) That in accordance with s.369(4) and s.378(3) of the Companies Act 1985 the Company hereby elects that the said provisions shall have effect as if the reference to 95 per cent were substituted by a reference to _____ per cent.[4]

(5) That the Company elects that the provisions of s.80A of Companies Act 1985 shall apply in relation to any giving or renewal after the passing of this resolution of an authority to allot shares pursuant to s.80 of that Act.

Directors' signatures: Date of each signature:

_____   _____

_____   _____

_____   _____

[1]Cannot be called on short notice.
[2]Any member still has the right to ask for an AGM.
[3]Accounts must still be prepared and sent out to members each year.
[4]This percentage cannot be reduced lower than 90%.

Form C47

Company Number: _____

THE COMPANIES ACT 1985
PRIVATE COMPANY LIMITED BY SHARES
WRITTEN RESOLUTION OF THE BOARD OF DIRECTORS

_____ LIMITED

Pursuant to the articles of association of the company, the undersigned, being all the directors of the company, hereby resolve:

THAT an extraordinary general meeting be convened to propose that the company be re-registered as a public company as defined in section 1(3) of the Companies Act 1985.[1]

Directors' signatures: Date of each signature:

_____   _____

_____   _____

_____   _____

[1] To re-register as a PLC a company must have an authorised share capital of at least £50,000 and in order to commence business must issue shares up to this amount and each share must be paid up at least as to 25% of its nominal value and the whole of any premium. The company must send to Companies House an application to re-register, a signed copy of the special resolution passed by the members, new memorandum and articles, a copy of the latest balance sheet, an unqualified auditors report on the latest balance sheet, a further report from the auditors stating that the company's net assets are not less than its capital as shown in the balance sheet and a statutory declaration from a director stating that the net asset position is maintained and the statutory requirements have been complied with. The company may not commence business as a PLC until it has received a certificate from the Companies House confirming that it may do so under section 117 Companies Act 1985.

Company Number: _____

THE COMPANIES ACT 1985
PRIVATE COMPANY LIMITED BY SHARES
WRITTEN RESOLUTION OF THE BOARD OF DIRECTORS

_____ LIMITED

Pursuant to the articles of association of the company, the undersigned, being all the directors of the company, hereby resolve:

THAT the registered office of the Company be changed to _____

_____

and the Secretary be instructed to file the necessary return with the Registrar of Companies.[1]

Directors' signatures: Date of each signature:

_____   _____

_____   _____

_____   _____

[1]File Companies House form 287. The registered address of the company cannot be changed outside the country stated in its memorandum of association.

Company Number: _____

THE COMPANIES ACT 1985
PRIVATE COMPANY LIMITED BY SHARES
WRITTEN RESOLUTION OF THE BOARD OF DIRECTORS

_____ **LIMITED**

Pursuant to the articles of association of the company, the undersigned, being all the directors of the company, hereby resolve:

THAT the seal, an impression of which is affixed to this resolution, be adopted as the common seal of the Company.[1]

Directors' signatures: Date of each signature:

_____   _____

_____   _____

_____   _____

[1]A company is not required to have a seal.

Company Number: _____

THE COMPANIES ACT 1985
PRIVATE COMPANY LIMITED BY SHARES
WRITTEN RESOLUTION OF THE BOARD OF DIRECTORS

_____ LIMITED

Pursuant to the articles of association of the company, the undersigned, being all the directors of the company, hereby resolve:

THAT the accounting reference date of the Company be changed from _____ to _____ and the Secretary be instructed to file the necessary return with Companies House.[1]

Directors' signatures: Date of each signature:

_____   _____

_____   _____

_____   _____

[1]*File Companies House form 225.*

Company Number: _____

THE COMPANIES ACT 1985
PRIVATE COMPANY LIMITED BY SHARES
WRITTEN RESOLUTION OF THE BOARD OF DIRECTORS

_____ LIMITED

Pursuant to the articles of association of the company, the undersigned, being all the directors of the company, hereby resolve:

THAT the company being unable to continue its business by reason of its liabilities an extraordinary general meeting be convened for the purpose of passing an extraordinary resolution to effect a creditors voluntary winding up of the company in accordance with section 84 of the Insolvency Act 1986.[1]

Directors' signatures: Date of each signature:

_____   _____

_____   _____

_____   _____

[1]*The directors must take expert advice from a licensed insolvency practitioner as soon as it appears that the company may be unable to continue its business by reason of its liabilities. There are serious criminal sanctions if a director fails to take every step to minimise the potential loss to the company's creditors once he knows or ought to have known that there is no reasonable prospect of the company avoiding an insolvent liquidation.*

Company Number: _____

THE COMPANIES ACT 1985
PRIVATE COMPANY LIMITED BY SHARES
WRITTEN RESOLUTION OF THE BOARD OF DIRECTORS

_____ LIMITED

Pursuant to the articles of association of the company, the undersigned, being all the directors of the company, hereby resolve:

THAT in accordance with section 94 of the Insolvency Act 1986 an extraordinary general meeting be convened for the purpose of passing an extraordinary resolution to effect a members' voluntary winding up of the company.[1]

Directors' signatures: Date of each signature:

_____   _____

_____   _____

_____   _____

[1]*The directors must make a statutory declaration as to the company's solvency within the period of 5 weeks prior to the EGM (see footnote to Form E17). The directors should take the advice of the company's auditors and a licensed insolvency practitioner before making the statutory declaration and passing this resolution. If they are unable to make such a declaration the winding up will be a creditors' voluntary winding up (see Form C52).*

Company Number: _____

THE COMPANIES ACT 1985
PRIVATE COMPANY LIMITED BY SHARES
WRITTEN RESOLUTION OF THE BOARD OF DIRECTORS

_____ LIMITED

Pursuant to the articles of association of the company, the undersigned, being all the directors of the company, hereby resolve:

THAT the company being/being likely to become unable to pay its debts an application be made to the court for an administration order, in order to achieve[2] _____

_____

_____

Directors' signatures: Date of each signature:

_____   _____

_____   _____

_____   _____

[1]The directors should take the advice of a licensed insolvency practitioner before passing this resolution. A petition to the court for an administration order must be supported by an affidavit and an independent report on the company's affairs. The order will only be granted if the court is satisfied that the company is or is likely to become unable to pay its debts and an order is likely to achieve one or more of the following: (a) the survival of the company, and the whole or any part of its undertaking as a going concern, (b) the approval of a voluntary arrangement with creditors, (c) the sanctioning of a scheme of arrangement under section 425 of Companies act 1985, and (d) a more advantageous realisation of the company's assets than would be effected on a winding up. Any creditor who has validly appointed an administrative receiver prior to the court's consideration of the petition must consent before an order can be made.
[2]Specify one or more of the outcomes listed in (a) to (d) in footnote 1 above.

Company Number: _____

THE COMPANIES ACT 1985
PRIVATE COMPANY LIMITED BY SHARES
WRITTEN RESOLUTION OF THE BOARD OF DIRECTORS

_____ LIMITED

Pursuant to the articles of association of the company, the undersigned, being all the directors of the company, hereby resolve:

THAT the remuneration of the auditors for the audit for the accounting period ended _____
be agreed at £ _____ inclusive of expenses.[1]

Directors' signatures: Date of each signature:

_____   _____

_____   _____

_____   _____

[1] The directors may only pass this resolution if they have been given the authority to do so by the members in general meeting.

Company Number: _____

THE COMPANIES ACT 1985
PRIVATE COMPANY LIMITED BY SHARES
WRITTEN RESOLUTION OF THE BOARD OF DIRECTORS

_____ LIMITED

Pursuant to the articles of association of the company, the undersigned, being all the directors of the company, hereby resolve:

THAT the remuneration of the auditors for services and advice for the accounting period ended _____

be agreed at £ _____ inclusive of expenses.

Directors' signatures: Date of each signature:

_____   _____

_____   _____

_____   _____

Company Number: _____

THE COMPANIES ACT 1985
PRIVATE COMPANY LIMITED BY SHARES
WRITTEN RESOLUTION OF THE BOARD OF DIRECTORS

_____ LIMITED

Pursuant to the articles of association of the company, the undersigned, being all the directors of the company, hereby resolve:

To instruct the Secretary to register the Company with H.M. Customs & Excise for VAT purposes.[1]

Directors' signatures: Date of each signature:

_____   _____

_____   _____

_____   _____

[1]Registration is obligatory if the company's taxable turnover in the past 12 months or less exceed £49,000, or if there are reasonable grounds for believing that its taxable turnover will exceed this amount in the next 30 days. The directors should take expert tax advice on this matter.

Company Number: _____

THE COMPANIES ACT 1985
PRIVATE COMPANY LIMITED BY SHARES
WRITTEN RESOLUTION OF THE BOARD OF DIRECTORS

_____ LIMITED

Pursuant to the articles of association of the company, the undersigned, being all the directors of the company, hereby resolve:

To issue a debenture dated _____

in favour of _____

on the terms produced to this meeting and that any director be authorised to execute such debenture on behalf of the company.[1]

Directors' signatures: Date of each signature:

_____   _____

_____   _____

_____   _____

[1] _It is the company's responsibility to register with Companies House any charge over the company's assets contained in the debenture within 21 days of the creation of the charge on Companies House form 395 . Details of the charge must also be entered in the company's register of charges._

Company Number: _____

THE COMPANIES ACT 1985
PRIVATE COMPANY LIMITED BY SHARES
WRITTEN RESOLUTION OF THE BOARD OF DIRECTORS

_____ LIMITED

Pursuant to the articles of association of the company, the undersigned, being all the directors of the company, hereby resolve:

THAT in accordance with section 320 of the Companies Act 1985 an extraordinary general meeting be convened to propose that the members approve a substantial property transaction involving _____ , being a director of the company, the terms of which are attached.[1]

Directors' signatures: Date of each signature:

_____   _____

_____   _____

_____   _____

[1]Section 320 of the Companies Act 1985 requires any arrangement between a company and a director involving the transfer, either from the company to the director or from the director to the company, of a non-cash asset the value of which exceeds £100,000 or 10% of the company's net assets (provided it is not less than £2,000) to be approved by the company's members.

Section D
General Meetings

The forms in this section are designed to be used in connection with a meeting of the company's shareholders. You should pay careful attention to the requirements relating to the notice periods for these meetings (see Introduction, page 4). You should also check the company's articles to make sure that the requirements for a quorum to be present and the correct voting procedures are observed.

The text of the actual resolutions you require may be selected from those set out in Section E and then inserted into the notices and minutes as appropriate. Where a document is referred to as being attached to the written resolution this should be replaced in the resolution in minute form by a reference to the relevant document being 'produced to the meeting'.

Section contents

Annual General Meeting

D01   Notice of Annual General Meeting—Announces the time, place and agenda of the annual general meeting. It must be given to all members entitled to attend 14 days prior to the meeting, or if a special resolution is proposed, 21 days. The basic agenda includes adopting accounts and reports of the directors and auditors, declaring a dividend, (re-)appointing auditors, electing directors, and confirming appointments to the board.

D02   Consent to short notice for an AGM—Members must give approval for an annual general meeting called on short notice.

D03   Appointment of a proxy for an AGM—A member allowed to vote at an annual meeting may appoint a non-member to vote in his place.

D04   Minutes of Annual General Meeting—An official recording of the proceedings at an annual general meeting.

Extraordinary General Meeting

D05   Notice of Extraordinary General Meeting—Announces the time, place and agenda of a general meeting that is not the annual general meeting. It must be given to all members entitled to attend 14 days prior to the meeting, or if a special resolution is proposed, 21 days.

D06   Consent to short notice for an EGM—Members must give approval for an extraordinary general meeting called on short notice.

D07   Appointment of proxy for an EGM—A member allowed to vote at an extraordinary meeting may appoint a non-member to vote in his place.

D08   Minutes of an Extraordinary General Meeting—An official recording of the proceedings at an extraordinary general meeting.

Other notices

D09   Special notice of resolution to remove a director—Notice to be given no later than 28 days prior to the date of the meeting to remove a director.

D10   Notice of meeting to remove a director—Notifies members of a general meeting to propose removal of a director.

D11   Notice of resolution given by the company to the director—Notifies the director being removed.

D12   Notice of meeting for elective resolution—Notifies members of a general meeting to propose an elective resolution.

D13   Special notice of resolution to remove auditors—Notice to be given to the company no later than 28 days prior to the date of the meeting to remove auditors before their term of office has expired.

D14   Notice of meeting to remove auditors—Notifies members of a general meeting to propose removal of auditors before their term of office has expired.

_____ LIMITED

NOTICE IS HEREBY GIVEN that the ANNUAL GENERAL MEETING of the above-named company will be held at _____

on _____ at _____ am/pm

for the following purposes.

1. To consider and adopt the company's accounts and reports of the directors and auditors for the period _____

   to _____ .

2. To declare a dividend.

3. To re-appoint _____

   as auditors of the company until the next general meeting at which accounts are laid before the company, at a fee to be agreed with the board of directors.

4. To elect directors in place of those retiring (see the directors report).

5. To confirm appointments to the board.

Dated

_____

By order of the board

_____

Secretary

Registered office: _____

A member entitled to attend and vote at the meeting convened by this Notice is entitled to appoint a proxy to attend and vote on a poll[1] in his/her place. A proxy need not be a member of the company.

[1] Unless the articles provide otherwise, a proxy may only vote on a poll.

_____ LIMITED

We, the undersigned, being all of the members of the company having a right to attend and vote at the annual general meeting of the company to be held on _____ at _____ am/pm., HEREBY CONSENT to the convening and holding of such meeting and the proposing and passing thereat of the resolutions set out in the notice of meeting notwithstanding that the meeting has been convened by less than the statutory period of notice.

Dated

_____

_____

_____

_____ LIMITED

NOTICE FORM OF PROXY FOR USE BY ORDINARY SHAREHOLDERS FOR THE ANNUAL GENERAL MEETING ON

_____

I _____ of _____being a member of the above-named company, hereby appoint _____ of _____ or, failing him/her, _____ of _____ or failing him/her the duly appointed chairman of the meeting as my proxy at the annual general meeting of the company to be held on _____ and at any adjournment thereof and to vote on my behalf as directed below.

RESOLUTIONS

		For	Against
1.	[*Insert text of resolution*][1]	☐	☐
2.	[*Insert text of resolution*]	☐	☐

Dated

_____

Signature

_____

Notes:
(a) This form of proxy, together with the power of attorney or other authority (if any) under which it was signed, or an office or notarially certified copy thereof, must be lodged [at the company's registered office] not later than 48 hours before the meeting.
(b) A proxy need not be a member of the company.
(c) In the case of joint holders the signature of the first-named will be accepted to the exclusion of all others.
(d) In the case of a corporation this form of proxy should be under its common seal or under the hand of an officer or attorney duly authorised.
(e) Any alterations to this form of proxy should be initialled.
(f) The completion of this form of proxy will not preclude the member from attending and voting in person if he/she so wishes.

[1] *For the text of various resolutions see Section E. Unless the articles provide otherwise, proxies may only vote on a poll.*

_____ LIMITED

MINUTES of the annual general meeting of the company held at

_____ on._____ at _____ a.m./p.m.

PRESENT _____ (in the chair)

IN ATTENDANCE _____

1. The Chairman announced that consents to the meeting being held at short notice had been received from all of the members of the company having a right to attend and vote at the meeting.

2. The Chairman declared that a quorum was present.

3. It was unanimously agreed that the notice convening the meeting should be taken as read.

4. The Chairman submitted the company's profit and loss account for the period ended _____ , together with the balance sheet as at that date and it was resolved that the accounts as submitted to the meeting be and are approved.[1]

5. It was resolved that a final dividend of _____ p per share in respect of the year ended _____ be declared on the ordinary shares of _____ each in the capital of the company, payable on _____ to the holders of ordinary shares registered at the close of business on _____.

6. It was resolved that _____ be re-appointed auditors of the company until the next general meeting at which accounts are laid before the company, at a fee to be agreed with the board of directors.

7. It was resolved that _____ , the director(s) retiring by rotation, be re-elected a director(s) of the company.

8. It was resolved that the appointment of _____ to the board on _____ be confirmed.

9. The meeting then ended.

_____

Chairman

[1]There is no requirement for the accounts to be approved by the shareholders; they need only be laid before them in general meeting - see Companies Act 1985 section 241.

_____ LIMITED

NOTICE IS HEREBY GIVEN that an EXTRAORDINARY GENERAL MEETING of the above-named company will be held at _____ on _____ at _____ am/pm to consider and, if thought fit, pass the following resolutions which will be proposed as to resolutions _____ as special resolutions and as to resolutions _____ as ordinary resolutions of the company.

SPECIAL RESOLUTIONS

[insert text of resolutions][1]_____

_____

ORDINARY RESOLUTION

[insert text of resolutions] _____

_____

Dated

_____

Signature

_____

A member entitled to attend and vote at the meeting convened by this Notice is entitled to appoint a proxy to attend and vote on a poll[2] in his/her place. A proxy need not be a member of the company.

1 For the text of various example resolutions see Section E
2 Unless the articles provide otherwise proxies may vote only on a poll.

Form D05

_____ LIMITED

We, the undersigned, being all of the members of the company having a right to attend and vote at the extraordinary general meeting of the company to be held on _____ at _____ am/pm., HEREBY CONSENT to the convening and holding of such meeting and the proposing and passing thereat of the resolutions set out in the notice of meeting notwithstanding that the meeting has been convened by less than the statutory period of notice.

Dated

_____

_____

_____

_____ LIMITED

FORM OF PROXY FOR USE BY ORDINARY SHAREHOLDERS
FOR THE EXTRAORDINARY GENERAL MEETING TO BE HELD ON

_____

I _____ of _____ being a member
of the above-named company, hereby appoint[2] _____
of _____ or, failing him/her, _____
of _____ or failing him/her the duly appointed
chairman of the meeting as my proxy at the extraordinary general meeting of the company to be held on _____
and at any adjournment thereof and to vote on my behalf as directed below.

RESOLUTIONS
Please indicate how you wish your proxy to vote by placing an 'X' in the
appropriate box. Unless otherwise indicated the proxy will exercise his
discretion as to how he votes and whether he abstains from voting.

		For	Against
1.	[*Insert text of resolution*][1]	☐	☐
2.	[*Insert text of resolution*]	☐	☐

Dated

_____

Signature

_____

Notes:
(a) This form of proxy, together with the power of attorney or other authority (if any) under which
     it was signed, or an office or notarially certified copy thereof, must be lodged [at the company's
     registered office] not later than 48 hours before the meeting.
(b) A proxy need not be a member of the company.
(c) In the case of joint holders the signature of the first-named will be accepted to the exclusion of
     all others.
(d) In the case of a corporation this form of proxy should be under its common seal or under the
     hand of an officer or attorney duly authorised.
(e) Any alterations to this form of proxy should be initialled.
(f) The completion of this form of proxy will not preclude the member from attending and voting
     in person if he/she so wishes.

[1] _For the text of various resolutions see Section E. Unless the articles provide otherwise, proxies may only vote
on a poll._

_____ LIMITED

MINUTES of an extraordinary general meeting of the company held at
_____ on _____ at _____ a.m./p.m.

PRESENT _____ (in the chair)

_____

IN ATTENDANCE _____

_____

1. The Chairman confirmed that notice of the meeting had been given to all the members of the company having a right to attend and vote at the meeting OR announced that consents to the meeting being held at short notice had been received from all of the members of the company having a right to attend and vote at the meeting .

2. The Chairman declared that a quorum was present.

3. It was unanimously agreed that the notice convening the meeting should be taken as read.

4. The Chairman proposed the following resolution as an ordinary/special resolution: _____

    _____

    _____

    _____

5. The Chairman put the resolution to the meeting, took the vote on a show of hands1 and declared the resolution passed as an ordinary/special resolution of the company.2

6. The meeting then ended.

_____

Chairman

1 If a poll is validly demanded, the resolution may not be passed or blocked on a show of hands. The circumstances in which a poll may be demanded and the way in which it should be conducted are set out in the articles (in Table A the relevant provisions are articles 46-52). The fact that a poll has been demanded, by whom and the result of the poll should be recorded in the minutes.
2 Repeat points 4 and 5 for each resolution.

_____ LIMITED

The Directors

_____

In accordance with sections 379 and 303(2) of the Companies Act 1985, I hereby give special notice of my intention to move the following resolution at a general meeting of the company, to be held not earlier than 28 days from the date of this notice.[1]

ORDINARY RESOLUTION

That _____

be and is hereby removed from office as a director of the company.

Dated

_____

_____

[1]This must be left at the company's registered office at least 28 days before the general meeting. On receipt of this notice the company must send a copy to the director concerned - see Form D11. The company must give notice of this resolution to the members when it gives them notice of the meeting (or, if that is not practicable, either by advertisement in a newspaper having an appropriate circulation or in any other mode allowed by the articles, not less than 21 days before the meeting) - see Form D10.

_____ LIMITED

NOTICE IS HEREBY GIVEN that an extraordinary general meeting of the company will be held at the registered office of the company on _____[1] at _____ am/pm to consider and, if thought fit, pass the following resolution as an ordinary resolution, special notice of this resolution having been given in accordance with sections 379 and 303(2) of the Companies Act 1985.[2]

ORDINARY RESOLUTION

That _____
be and is hereby removed from office as a director of the company.

Dated

_____

By order of the board

_____

Secretary

Registered office:_____

A member entitled to attend and vote at the meeting convened by this Notice is entitled to appoint a proxy to attend and vote [on a poll]3 in his/her place. A proxy need not be a member of the company.

[1] Date of meeting must be at least 28 days after date of receipt of special notice.
[2] If the company has received any representations from the director in respect of his removal this notice should state this fact and a copy of the representations should be sent to all the shareholders. File Companies House form 288b after passing of resolution.
[3] Unless the articles provide otherwise, proxies may vote only on a poll.

_____ LIMITED

To:

Date:

Dear Sir

I am writing to inform you that the enclosed special notice has been received, in accordance with section 303 of the Companies Act 1985, and that the following ordinary resolution will be proposed at an extraordinary general meeting of the company on _____ at _____ am/pm at the registered office of this company.

ORDINARY RESOLUTION

That _____ be and is hereby removed from office as director of the company.

In accordance with section 304 of the Companies Act 1985 you are entitled to be heard at the meeting and may request that representations in writing made by you be sent to all members of the company to whom notices of the meetings are sent. If you wish representations to be sent may I receive them not later than _____.

Yours faithfully

_____

[1] _Send as soon as special notice is received. Enclose a copy of the special notice._

_____ LIMITED

NOTICE IS HEREBY GIVEN that an extraordinary general meeting of the above-named company will be held at _____ on the _____ , at _____ am/pm for the purpose of considering, and if thought fit, passing the following resolution(s) which is/are proposed as an elective resolution(s):

ELECTIVE RESOLUTION(S)

1. _____

2. _____

Dated

_____

By order of the board

_____

Secretary

Registered office: _____

A member entitled to attend and vote at this meeting is entitled to appoint a proxy, who does not have to be a member of the company, to attend and vote [on a poll][1] for him.

---

[1] Unless the articles provide otherwise, a proxy may only vote on a poll.

_____ LIMITED

The Directors

_____

In accordance with sections 379 and 391A of the Companies Act 1985, I hereby give special notice of my intention to move the following resolution at a general meeting of the company, to be held not earlier than 28 days from the date of this notice.[1]

ORDINARY RESOLUTION

That _____
be and are hereby removed from their office as auditors of the company.

Dated

_____

_____

_____

[1]_This must be left at the company's registered office at least 28 days before the general meeting. On receipt of this notice the company must send a copy to the auditors see Form C08. The company must give notice of this resolution to the members when it gives them notice of the meeting see Form D14 (or, if that is not practicable, either by advertisement in a newspaper having an appropriate circulation or in any other mode allowed by the articles, not less than 21 days before the meeting)._

_____ LIMITED

NOTICE IS HEREBY GIVEN that an extraordinary general meeting of the company will be held at the registered office of the company on _____[1] at _____ am/pm to consider and, if thought fit, pass the following resolution as an ordinary resolution, special notice of this resolution having been given in accordance with sections 379 and 391A of the Companies Act 1985.[2]

ORDINARY RESOLUTION

That _____

be and are hereby removed from their office as auditors of the company.

Dated

_____

By order of the board

_____

Secretary

Registered office:_____

A member entitled to attend and vote at the meeting convened by this Notice is entitled to appoint a proxy to attend and vote [on a poll][3] in his/her place. A proxy need not be a member of the company.

[1]Date of meeting must be at least 28 days from date of receipt of special notice.
[2]If the company has received any representations from the auditors in respect of their removal this notice should state this fact and a copy of the representations should be sent to all the shareholders. File Companies House form 391 within 14 days of passing resolution.
[3]Unless the articles provide otherwise, proxies may vote only on a poll.

Section E

Shareholders' Resolutions

Shareholders' resolutions are classified as ordinary, special, extraordinary or elective, depending on their intention. An ordinary resolution (OR) requires a majority approval (i.e. more than 50 per cent). A special resolution (SR) or an extraordinary resolution (XR) requires a three-quarters majority of the votes cast at a meeting, which requires at least 21 clear days' notice. An elective resolution (ER) requires consent of all shareholders entitled to vote. Shareholders resolutions may be passed at annual or extraordinary general meetings or by passing a written resolution, as provided in this section. The company number is written on the certificate of incorporation you received from the Companies House.

Passing the written resolution

If the written resolution procedure is used the directors must notify the company's auditors of the contents of the resolution or send them a copy of it at or before the time it is supplied to the members for signature, unless the articles permit a written resolution to be passed and do not require the auditors to be notified in this way. A written resolution must be signed by all the members (although they may sign separate copies) irrespective of whether it is an ordinary, special or elective resolution. It becomes effective on the signature of the last member and should be dated with the date on which that member signed.

The company will be empowered to pass a written resolution by one of three authorities:

(a) if the company's articles incorporate regulation 53 of Table A, by that regulation; or

(b) if the company's articles do not incorporate regulation 53 of Table A but contain authority to pass written resolutions in another article; or

(c) by section 381A of the Companies Act 1985; this gives the company a power to pass a written resolution in addition to any power which may be contained in its articles.

You will see that each from in this section offers you these three options as your authority for passing a written resolution. If you wish to rely on a power in the company's articles you should check your company's articles to see whether option (a) or (b) above is appropriate. Alternatively, you may rely on the power in section 381A irrespective of whether the articles contain a separate power or not. You should note however that you will only be able to dispense with the obligation to notify the company's auditors of the resolution (see above) if you rely on a provision of your company's articles as authority to pass the resolution and that provision does not require the auditors to be notified. Once you have selected the appropriate option you should delete the other two.

You will also notice that in some of the forms Table A is referred to in the text of the resolution itself. This is the case, for example, in those forms which amend the company's articles of association (E39-48). Before using these forms you should check that your company's articles incorporate the particular regulations of Table A referred to. If they do not these forms will not be appropriate for use by your company.

After the resolution has been passed

Once the written resolution has been passed, it should be placed in the company's minute book. Certain resolutions should filed at Companies House e.g. all elective and special resolutions and some ordinary resolutions, such as the giving of authority to allot shares under section 80 Companies Act 1985. Where this is required a separate print of a resolution passed at a meeting should be prepared and signed by the chairman, while if a written resolution has been passed the filing of a copy of the signed document will generally suffice.

Section contents

E01   Standard written resolution—This is the basic format for a shareholders' resolution to be passed without holding a general meeting.

Appointments and Removals

E02   Appointment of director (OR)—Resolves to appoint a new director.

E03   Fixing of maximum number of directors (OR)—Resolves to limit the number of directors.

Shares

E04   Increase of authorised share capital (OR)—Resolves to increase the company's authorised share capital by creating new shares.

E05 Reduction of share capital (SR)—Resolves to reduce share capital by dividing shares and reducing the nominal amount of each share.

E06 Allotment of shares - specific authority (OR)—Resolves to give directors authority to make a specific allotment of a certain number for a specified purpose.

E07 Allotment of shares - general authority (OR)—Resolves to give directors general and unconditional authority to allot a certain number of shares for a period of up to five years or, if the relevant elective resolution is in place (see Form E20), for an indefinite period.

E08 Removal of authority to allot shares (OR)—Resolves to revoke directors' authority to allot ordinary shares

E09 Declaration of dividend (OR)—Resolves to pay shareholders a dividend.

E10 Removal of statutory pre-emption rights - general (SR)—Resolves to remove the statutory right of existing shareholders to be offered any new shares which are to be allotted before they are allotted to anyone else, in respect of any allotment made pursuant to a general section 80 authority conferred on the directors (see Form E07).

E11 Removal of statutory pre-emption rights in respect of specified allotment (SR)—Resolves to remove the right of existing shareholders to be offered any new shares which are to be allotted before they are allotted to anyone else in respect of a specified allotment.

E12 Purchase of own shares (SR)—Resolves to approve the company's purchase of shares otherwise than out of capital.

E13 Purchase of own shares from capital (SR)—Resolves to approve the company's purchase of shares out of capital.

E14 Bonus issue (OR)—Resolves to issue shares by way of bonus issue.

Financial

E15 Approval of substantial property transaction (OR)—Resolves to approve a substantial property transaction involving a director.

E16   Approval of directors' remuneration (OR)—Resolves to pay a director a designated amount.

E17   Voluntary liquidation - solvent (SR)—Resolves to begin the winding up of the company.

E18   Voluntary liquidation - insolvent (XR)—Resolves to begin winding up because the company is insolvent and unable to pay its debts.

E19   Application for administration order (OR)—Resolves to apply for an administrator to be appointed to run the company while it is unable to pay its debts.

Elective Resolutions

E20   Authority to allot shares for period greater than five-year maximum (ER)—Resolves to allow directors to allot shares for greater than a 5-year period.

E21   Removal of need to lay accounts before members (ER)—Resolves to remove the need to lay accounts before members.

E22   Removal of need for AGM (ER)—Resolves to remove the requirement to hold an annual general meeting.

E23   Removal of requirement to re-elect auditor (ER)—Resolves to remove the requirement to re-appoint auditors on an annual basis.

E24   Decrease of percentage shareholding required to consent to short notice (ER)—Resolves to decrease the percentage shareholding required to consent to holding a meeting on short notice.

Remove Elective Resolutions

E25   Re-establishment of 5-year maximum to allot shares (OR)—Resolves to remove the elective resolution which allots shares for greater than a 5-year period.

E26   Re-establishment of need to lay accounts before members (OR)—Resolves to remove the elective resolution which removes the need to lay accounts before members.

E27   Re-establishment of need for AGM (OR)—Resolves to remove the elective resolution which removes the need for an annual general meeting.

E28   Re-establishment of requirement to re-elect auditor (OR)—Resolves to remove the elective resolution which removes the need to appoint auditors on an annual basis.

E29   Re-establishment of percentage shareholding required to consent to short notice (OR)—Resolves to remove the elective resolution which decreases the percentage shareholding required to consent to holding a meeting on short notice.

Change Constitution

E30   Re-registration as public company (SR)—Resolves to re-register company as a public company.

E31   Change of company name (SR)—Resolves to change the company name.

E32   Change of articles (SR)—Resolves to alter certain articles of association.

E33   Adoption of new articles of association (SR)—Resolves to replace entire articles of association.

E34   Change of objects (SR)—Resolves to alter certain objects of the company as set out in the memorandum of association.

Directors

E35   Approval of compensation payment (OR)—Resolves to approve payment to a retiring director.

E36   Approval of service contract exceeding five years' duration (OR)—Resolves to approve a director's service contract of more than five years.

E37   Ratification of acts of directors beyond the powers delegated to them under the articles (OR)—Resolves to ratify acts of directors which were beyond the powers delegated to them.

E38   Allowing of director to vote on contracts where has personal interest (OR)—Resolves to approve a director voting on a matter in which he has a personal interest.

Altering the articles

E39   Alteration of articles - no retirement by rotation (OR)—changes articles so that directors are not required to retire by rotation.

E40   Alteration of articles - removal of chairman's casting vote (OR)—changes articles so that the chairman does not have a casting vote at board meetings.

E41   Alteration of articles - director voting where personal interest (OR)—changes articles so that a director can vote at a any meeting or on any resolution where he has a personal interest.

E42   Alteration of articles - refusal to register transfer of shares (OR)—changes articles so that directors have discretion to refuse to register a transfer of ownership of shares.

E43   Alteration of articles - exclusion of statutory pre-emption rights (OR)—changes articles so that the statutory rights of existing shareholders to be offered any shares which are to be allotted - before they are allotted to anyone else - are excluded.

E44   Alteration of articles - quorum for general meeting (OR)—changes articles so that if a quorum is not present at a general meeting the meeting be adjourned.

E45   Alteration of articles - number of directors (OR)—changes articles so that maximum and minimum numbers of directors may be varied.

E46   Alteration of articles - alternate directors (OR)—changes articles so that directors may specify that a proportion of their remuneration is paid to their alternate.

E47   Alteration of articles - weighted voting rights (OR)—changes articles so that directors (assuming they are shareholders) have weighted voting rights in order to prevent themselves from being removed from office.

E48   Alteration of articles - authority to allot shares (OR)—changes articles so that directors have authority to allot shares.

Company Number: _____

THE COMPANIES ACT 1985
PRIVATE COMPANY LIMITED BY SHARES
WRITTEN RESOLUTION

OF

_____ LIMITED

passed on _____

In accordance with [section 381A of the Companies Act 1985]/[article _____ of the company's articles of association]/[regulation 53 of Table A, which is incorporated in the company's articles of association by virtue of article [1] of those articles] we, the undersigned, being all the members of the company who, at the date of this resolution would be entitled to attend and vote at general meetings of the company, hereby unanimously resolve upon the following resolutions and agree that they shall be as valid and effective as if they had been passed as [an ordinary/elective/extraordinary/a special] resolution (in the case of resolution 1) and [a special/an ordinary/elective/extraordinary] resolution (in the case of resolution 2) at a general meeting of the company duly convened and held.

[insert text of resolutions] _____

_____

Dated

_____

_____

_____

Notes:
  •The directors must notify the company's auditors of the contents of the resolution at or before the time the resolution is supplied to the members (failure to do so can result in a fine) unless the company does not have an auditor(in which case they can still use the written resolution procedure) or the articles permit a written resolution to be passed and do not require auditors.
  •A written resolution must be signed by all members and whether there is an auditor to notify or not the resolution will be effective on the signature of the last member.
  •The written resolution procedure cannot be used in two specified circumstances: a resolution to remove a director before the expiration of his period of office (under section 303 Companies Act 1985) and a resolution to remove an auditor before the expiration of his term of office (under section 391 Companies Act 1985).

Company Number: _____

THE COMPANIES ACT 1985
PRIVATE COMPANY LIMITED BY SHARES
WRITTEN RESOLUTION

OF

_____ LIMITED

passed on _____

In accordance with [section 381A of the Companies Act 1985]/[article _____ of the company's articles of association]/[regulation 53 of Table A, which is incorporated in the company's articles of association by virtue of article [1] of those articles] we, the undersigned, being all the members of the company who, at the date of this resolution would be entitled to attend and vote at general meetings of the company, hereby unanimously resolve upon the following resolution and agree that it shall be as valid and effective as if it had been passed as an ordinary resolution at a general meeting of the company duly convened and held.

THAT _____ be appointed a director of the company[1]

Dated

_____

_____

_____

[1]File Companies House form 288a. Alter register of directors and if new director is interested in shares in the company (see section 324 Companies Act 1985) update the register of directors' interests.

Company Number: _____

THE COMPANIES ACT 1985
PRIVATE COMPANY LIMITED BY SHARES
WRITTEN RESOLUTION

OF

_____ LIMITED

passed on _____

In accordance with [section 381A of the Companies Act 1985]/[article _____of the company's articles of association]/[regulation 53 of Table A, which is incorporated in the company's articles of association by virtue of article [1] of those articles] we, the undersigned, being all the members of the company who, at the date of this resolution would be entitled to attend and vote at general meetings of the company, hereby unanimously resolve upon the following resolution and agree that it shall be as valid and effective as if it had been passed as an ordinary resolution at a general meeting of the company duly convened and held.

That the maximum number of directors of the company shall be _____.[1]

Dated

_____

_____

_____

[1]Table A regulation 64 states that unless otherwise determined by ordinary resolution, the number of directors (other than alternate directors) shall not be subject to any maximum but shall not be less than two.

Company Number: _____

THE COMPANIES ACT 1985
PRIVATE COMPANY LIMITED BY SHARES
WRITTEN RESOLUTION

OF

_____ LIMITED

passed on _____

In accordance with [section 381A of the Companies Act 1985]/[article _____ of the company's articles of association]/[regulation 53 of Table A, which is incorporated in the company's articles of association by virtue of article [1] of those articles] we, the undersigned, being all the members of the company who, at the date of this resolution would be entitled to attend and vote at general meetings of the company, hereby unanimously resolve upon the following resolution and agree that it shall be as valid and effective as if it had been passed as an ordinary resolution at a general meeting of the company duly convened and held.

That the authorised share capital of the company be increased from £ _____ to £ _____ by the creation of an additional _____ ordinary shares of _____ each to rank pari passu in all respects with the capital of the company.[1]

Dated

_____

_____

_____

[1]Share capital can only be increased if the articles allow it. Regulation 32 of Table A does. File the resolution, the amended memorandum and Companies House form 123 at Companies House. The notice of the meeting must state the amount of the increase.

Company Number: _____

THE COMPANIES ACT 1985
PRIVATE COMPANY LIMITED BY SHARES
WRITTEN RESOLUTION

OF

_____ LIMITED

passed on _____

In accordance with [section 381A of the Companies Act 1985]/[article _____ of the company's articles of association]/[regulation 53 of Table A, which is incorporated in the company's articles of association by virtue of article [1] of those articles] we, the undersigned, being all the members of the company who, at the date of this resolution would be entitled to attend and vote at general meetings of the company, hereby unanimously resolve upon the following resolution and agree that it shall be as valid and effective as if it had been passed as a special resolution at a general meeting of the company duly convened and held.

That in accordance with section 135 Companies Act 1985 the authorised share capital of the company be reduced[1] from £ _____ , divided into _____ ordinary shares of [£1] each to £_____ , divided into _____ ordinary shares of [50p] each, and that such reduction be effected by cancelling paid up capital to the extent of [50p] on each of the shares of [£1] each in the capital of the company and reducing the nominal amount of each share whether issued or unissued from [£1] to [50p] accordingly.[2]

Dated

_____

_____

_____

[1]The rules governing a company's ability to reduce its share capital are complex and the procedure involves obtaining the consent of the court. This resolution should not therefore be used without first taking the advice of the company's solicitors.
[2]File resolution with Companies House.

Company Number: _____

THE COMPANIES ACT 1985
PRIVATE COMPANY LIMITED BY SHARES
WRITTEN RESOLUTION

OF

_____ **LIMITED**

passed on _____

In accordance with [section 381A of the Companies Act 1985]/[article _____ of the company's articles of association]/[regulation 53 of Table A, which is incorporated in the company's articles of association by virtue of article [1] of those articles] we, the undersigned, being all the members of the company who, at the date of this resolution would be entitled to attend and vote at general meetings of the company, hereby unanimously resolve upon the following resolution and agree that it shall be as valid and effective as if it had been passed as an ordinary resolution at a general meeting of the company duly convened and held.

That in accordance with section 80 of the Companies Act 1985 the members authorise the directors to allot, or to grant any right to subscribe for or to convert any security into up to _____ ordinary shares of £ _____ each in the capital of the company for the purposes of _____ provided that such authority shall expire _____ months/years[1] from the date of the passing of the resolution and that the directors may make an offer or agreement before the expiry of such authority which would or might require shares to be allotted after the expiry of such authority.[2]

Dated

_____

_____

_____

Company Number: _____

THE COMPANIES ACT 1985
PRIVATE COMPANY LIMITED BY SHARES
WRITTEN RESOLUTION

OF

_____ LIMITED

passed on _____

In accordance with [section 381A of the Companies Act 1985]/[article _____ of the company's articles of association]/[regulation 53 of Table A, which is incorporated in the company's articles of association by virtue of article [1] of those articles] we, the undersigned, being all the members of the company who, at the date of this resolution would be entitled to attend and vote at general meetings of the company, hereby unanimously resolve upon the following resolution and agree that it shall be as valid and effective as if it had been passed as an ordinary resolution at a general meeting of the company duly convened and held.[1]

That in accordance with section 80 of the Companies Act 1985 the members generally and unconditionally authorise the directors to allot, or to grant any right to subscribe for or to convert any security into up to _____ ordinary shares of _____ each in the capital of the company provided that such authority shall expire _____ months/years from the date of the passing of this resolution[2] and that the directors may make an offer or agreement before the expiry of such authority which would or might require shares to be allotted after the expiry of such authority.

Dated

_____

_____

_____

[1] File resolution with Companies House
[2] The maximum period for which this authority may be given is five years but if the company has previously passed the relevant elective resolution (see Form E20) this authority may be given for an indefinite period.

Form E07

Company Number: _____

THE COMPANIES ACT 1985
PRIVATE COMPANY LIMITED BY SHARES
WRITTEN RESOLUTION

OF

_____ LIMITED

passed on _____

In accordance with [section 381A of the Companies Act 1985]/[article _____ of the company's articles of association]/[regulation 53 of Table A, which is incorporated in the company's articles of association by virtue of article [1] of those articles] we, the undersigned, being all the members of the company who, at the date of this resolution would be entitled to attend and vote at general meetings of the company, hereby unanimously resolve upon the following resolution and agree that it shall be as valid and effective as if it had been passed as an ordinary resolution at a general meeting of the company duly convened and held.

That in accordance with section 80 of the Companies Act 1985 the members hereby revoke the directors' authority to issue ordinary shares conferred on them by a resolution dated_____.

Dated

_____

_____

_____

Company Number: _____

THE COMPANIES ACT 1985
PRIVATE COMPANY LIMITED BY SHARES
WRITTEN RESOLUTION

OF

_____ LIMITED

passed on _____

In accordance with [section 381A of the Companies Act 1985]/[article _____ of the Company's articles of association]/[regulation 53 of Table A, which is incorporated in the Company's articles of association by virtue of article [1] of those articles] we, the undersigned, being all the members of the Company who, at the date of this resolution would be entitled to attend and vote at general meetings of the Company, hereby unanimously resolve upon the following resolution and agree that it shall be as valid and effective as if it had been passed as an ordinary resolution at a general meeting of the company duly convened and held.

That a dividend of _____p per share in respect of the year ended _____ be declared on the ordinary shares of _____ each in the capital of the Company, payable on _____ to the holders of ordinary shares registered at the close of business on _____ .[1]

Dated

_____

_____

_____

[1] *Under Table A regulation 102 shareholders cannot decide to pay themselves more than the directors have recommended, but they can decide to pay themselves less.*

Company Number: _____

THE COMPANIES ACT 1985
PRIVATE COMPANY LIMITED BY SHARES
WRITTEN RESOLUTION

OF

_____ LIMITED

passed on _____

In accordance with [section 381A of the Companies Act 1985]/[article _____ of the company's articles of association]/[regulation 53 of Table A, which is incorporated in the company's articles of association by virtue of article [1] of those articles] we, the undersigned, being all the members of the company who, at the date of this resolution would be entitled to attend and vote at general meetings of the company, hereby unanimously resolve upon the following resolution and agree that it shall be as valid and effective as if it had been passed as a special resolution at a general meeting of the company duly convened and held.

That in accordance with section 95 of the Companies Act 1985, section 89(1) of that Act shall not apply to the allotment of shares pursuant to the general authority given under section 80 of that Act by a resolution of the company dated _____ and the directors may allot, grant options over or otherwise dispose of such shares to such persons, on such terms and in such manner as they see fit.[1]

Dated

_____

_____

_____

[1] *File resolution with Companies House.*

Company Number: _____

THE COMPANIES ACT 1985
PRIVATE COMPANY LIMITED BY SHARES
WRITTEN RESOLUTION

OF

_____ LIMITED

passed on _____

In accordance with [section 381A of the Companies Act 1985]/[article _____ of the company's articles of association]/[regulation 53 of Table A, which is incorporated in the company's articles of association by virtue of article [1] of those articles] we, the undersigned, being all the members of the company who, at the date of this resolution would be entitled to attend and vote at general meetings of the company, hereby unanimously resolve upon the following resolution and agree that it shall be as valid and effective as if it had been passed as a special resolution at a general meeting of the company duly convened and held.

That in accordance with section 95 of the Companies Act 1985, section 89(1) of that Act shall not apply to the allotment of shares for the purposes of _____ pursuant to the authority given under section 80 of that Act[1] by a resolution of the company dated _____.

Dated

_____

_____

_____

[1] *File resolution with Companies House. With the written resolution or the notice of meeting directors must send to members a written statement setting out their reasons for recommending this resolution, the amount to be paid to the company on the allotment and their justification for that amount. There are serious penalties if the directors issue a false, misleading or deceptive statement in these circumstances.*

Form E11

Company Number: _____

THE COMPANIES ACT 1985
PRIVATE COMPANY LIMITED BY SHARES
WRITTEN RESOLUTION

OF

_____ LIMITED

passed on _____

In accordance with [section 381A of the Companies Act 1985]/[article _____ of the company's articles of association]/[regulation 53 of Table A, which is incorporated in the company's articles of association by virtue of article [1] of those articles] we, the undersigned, being all the members of the company who, at the date of this resolution would be entitled to attend and vote at general meetings of the company, hereby unanimously resolve upon the following resolution and agree that it shall be as valid and effective as if it had been passed as a special resolution at a general meeting of the company duly convened and held.[1]

That in accordance with section 162 of the Companies Act 1985 the proposed contract for the purchase by the company of shares in the company held by _____, a copy of which is attached to this resolution and marked 'A' for the purposes of identification, be approved.[2]

Dated

_____

_____

_____

[1]The purchase by a company of its own shares is allowed only in certain limited circumstances and the directors should not propose this resolution without first seeking the advice of the company's auditors and shareholders should take advice on the tax treatment of the money paid to them.
[2]The articles must allow this. The contract must be available for inspection at the registered office for ten years after the passing of the resolution. File Companies House form G169 and a copy of this resolution with Companies House ,stating the number of shares and their nominal value. Amend the register of members. N.B. If this resolution is to be used at an EGM delete reference to a copy of the contract being attached. The contract should instead be available for inspection at the registered office for 15 days before the meeting and at the meeting itself.

Company Number: _____

THE COMPANIES ACT 1985
PRIVATE COMPANY LIMITED BY SHARES
WRITTEN RESOLUTION

OF

_____ LIMITED

passed on _____

In accordance with [section 381A of the Companies Act 1985]/[article _____ of the company's articles of association]/[regulation 53 of Table A, which is incorporated in the company's articles of association by virtue of article [1] of those articles] we, the undersigned, being all the members of the company who, at the date of this resolution would be entitled to attend and vote at general meetings of the company, hereby unanimously resolve upon the following resolution and agree that it shall be as valid and effective as if it had been passed as a special resolution at a general meeting of the company duly convened and held.[1]

That in accordance with section 171 of the Companies Act 1985 the proposed contract for the purchase by the company of shares in the company held by _____ a copy of which is attached to this resolution and marked 'A' for the purposes of identification be approved and that such purchase be financed out of capital.[2]

Dated

_____

_____

_____

[1]A company may only purchase its own shares out of capital (i.e. otherwise than from distributable profits or the proceeds of a fresh issue of shares) as a last resort. The rules governing such a purchase and the tax treatment of money paid to shareholders are complex and this resolution should not be proposed without first seeking the advice of the company's auditors and solicitors.
[2]The articles must allow this. The contract must be available for inspection at the registered office fifteen days before the meeting, at the meeting and for ten years afterwards. Companies House form G169 and a copy of this resolution should be filed with Companies House stating the number of shares and their nominal value. Amend the register of members. Creditors must be notified by means of a notice in the London Gazette (tel 0171 394 4580) and a national newspaper, the directors must make a statutory declaration of solvency supported by a report given by the company's auditors.
N.B. If this resolution is to be used at an EGM delete reference to a copy of the contract being attached. The contract should instead be available for inspection at the registered office for 15 days before the meeting and at the meeting itself.

Form E13

Company Number: _____

THE COMPANIES ACT 1985
PRIVATE COMPANY LIMITED BY SHARES
WRITTEN RESOLUTION

OF

_____ LIMITED

passed on _____

In accordance with [section 381A of the Companies Act 1985]/[article _____ of the company's articles of association]/[regulation 53 of Table A, which is incorporated in the company's articles of association by virtue of article [1] of those articles] we, the undersigned, being all the members of the company who, at the date of this resolution would be entitled to attend and vote at general meetings of the company, hereby unanimously resolve upon the following resolution and agree that it shall be as valid and effective as if it had been passed as an ordinary resolution at a general meeting of the company duly convened and held.

That the directors be authorised to capitalise the sum of £ _____ being part of the undivided profits of the company standing to the credit of the [profit and loss account] and to appropriate such sum to the holders of the ordinary shares of £1 each in the capital of the company as appearing in the register of members as at the close of business on _____ and that the directors be authorised and directed to apply such sum in paying up in full _____ shares of £1 each in the capital of the company and to allot and distribute such new shares, credited as fully paid, to the holders of the shares in proportion to their existing holdings of ordinary shares of £1 each.

Dated

_____

_____

_____

Company Number: _____

THE COMPANIES ACT 1985
PRIVATE COMPANY LIMITED BY SHARES
WRITTEN RESOLUTION

OF

_____ LIMITED

passed on _____

In accordance with [section 381A of the Companies Act 1985]/[article _____ of the company's articles of association]/[regulation 53 of Table A, which is incorporated in the company's articles of association by virtue of article [1] of those articles] we, the undersigned, being all the members of the company who, at the date of this resolution would be entitled to attend and vote at general meetings of the company, hereby unanimously resolve upon the following resolution and agree that it shall be as valid and effective as if it had been passed as an ordinary resolution at a general meeting of the company duly convened and held.

That in accordance with section 320 of the Companies Act 1985 the members approve the following transaction between the company and _____, a director of the company/a person connected with a director of the company.[1]

Dated

_____

_____

_____

[1]Section 320 of the Companies Act requires any arrangement between a company and a director involving the transfer, either from the company to the director or from the director to the company, of a non-cash asset the value of which exceeds £100,000 or 10% of the company's net assets (provided it is not less than £2000) to be approved by the company's members.

Company Number: _____

THE COMPANIES ACT 1985
PRIVATE COMPANY LIMITED BY SHARES
WRITTEN RESOLUTION

OF

_____ LIMITED

passed on _____

In accordance with [section 381A of the Companies Act 1985]/[article _____ of the company's articles of association]/[regulation 53 of Table A, which is incorporated in the company's articles of association by virtue of article [1] of those articles] we, the undersigned, being all the members of the company who, at the date of this resolution would be entitled to attend and vote at general meetings of the company, hereby unanimously resolve upon the following resolution and agree that it shall be as valid and effective as if it had been passed as an ordinary resolution at a general meeting of the company duly convened and held.

That the payment of £ _____ be paid to _____ as remuneration on a _____ basis be approved.

Dated

_____

_____

_____

Company Number: _____

THE COMPANIES ACT 1985
PRIVATE COMPANY LIMITED BY SHARES
WRITTEN RESOLUTION

OF

_____ LIMITED

passed on _____

In accordance with [section 381A of the Companies Act 1985]/[article _____ of the company's articles of association]/[regulation 53 of Table A, which is incorporated in the company's articles of association by virtue of article [1] of those articles] we, the undersigned, being all the members of the company who, at the date of this resolution would be entitled to attend and vote at general meetings of the company, hereby unanimously resolve upon the following resolutions and agree that they shall be as valid and effective as if they had been passed as regards resolution no. 1 as a special resolution and as regards resolution no. 2 as an ordinary resolution at a general meeting of the company duly convened and held.[1]

1. That in accordance with section 84 of the Insolvency Act 1986, the Company being solvent, proceedings be initiated to effect a members' voluntary winding up.[2]

2. That _____ be appointed as liquidator of the Company in accordance with section 91 of the Insolvency Act 1986.

Dated

_____

_____

_____

[1] A statutory declaration of solvency must be made by the directors (or, if there are more than two directors, by a majority of them), at a board meeting, that they have made a full inquiry into the company's affairs and, having done so, have formed the opinion that the company will be able to pay its debts in full together with interest at the official rate (as set out in section 251 of the Insolvency Act 1986) within a period not exceeding 12 months from the commencement of the winding up. The declaration must be made within the five week period immediately preceding the passing of this resolution. It must be filed with Companies House within 15 days of the passing of the resolution. N.B. The directors should not make this declaration without taking the advice of the company's auditors and a licensed insolvency practitioner.
[2] The special resolution must be advertised in the London Gazette within 14 days and filed with Companies House.

Company Number: _____

THE COMPANIES ACT 1985
PRIVATE COMPANY LIMITED BY SHARES
WRITTEN RESOLUTION

OF

_____ LIMITED

passed on _____

In accordance with [section 381A of the Companies Act 1985]/[article _____ of the company's articles of association]/[regulation 53 of Table A, which is incorporated in the company's articles of association by virtue of article [1] of those articles] we, the undersigned, being all the members of the company who, at the date of this resolution would be entitled to attend and vote at general meetings of the company, hereby unanimously resolve upon the following resolution and agree that it shall be as valid and effective as if it had been passed as an extraordinary resolution at a general meeting of the company duly convened and held.

That, the company being unable to continue its business by reason of its liabilities[1], proceedings be initiated to effect a creditors' voluntary winding up, in accordance with section 84 of the Insolvency Act 1986.[2]

Dated

_____

_____

_____

[1]The directors must take expert advice from a licensed insolvency practitioner as soon as it appears that the company may be unable to continue its business by reason of its liabilities.
[2]The resolution must be advertised in the London Gazette within 14 days and filed with Companies House. A meeting of the company's creditors must be called within 14 days of the passing of the resolution and the creditors given at least seven days' notice of such meeting. The company should take legal advice concerning the contents of the notice to creditors and the procedure to be followed generally.

Company Number: _____

THE COMPANIES ACT 1985
PRIVATE COMPANY LIMITED BY SHARES
WRITTEN RESOLUTION

OF

_____ LIMITED

passed on _____

In accordance with [section 381A of the Companies Act 1985]/[article _____ of the company's articles of association]/[regulation 53 of Table A, which is incorporated in the company's articles of association by virtue of article [1] of those articles] we, the undersigned, being all the members of the company who, at the date of this resolution would be entitled to attend and vote at general meetings of the company, hereby unanimously resolve upon the following resolution and agree that it shall be as valid and effective as if it had been passed as an ordinary resolution at a general meeting of the company duly convened and held.

That in accordance with section 9 of the Insolvency Act 1986 the company being/being likely to become unable[1] to pay its debts petition the court for an administration order in order to achieve

_____.[2,3]

Dated

_____

_____

_____

[1]Delete as appropriate.
[2]Specify one of more of the outcomes (a) - (d) listed in footnote on Form C54.
[3]The resolution must be advertised in the London Gazette within 14 days. Although the shareholders may pass this resolution, it is more usual for an application to be instigated by the directors without obtaining the approval of the shareholders (see Form C54).

Company Number: _____

THE COMPANIES ACT 1985
PRIVATE COMPANY LIMITED BY SHARES
WRITTEN RESOLUTION

OF

_____ LIMITED

passed on _____

In accordance with [section 381A of the Companies Act 1985]/[article _____ of the company's articles of association]/[regulation 53 of Table A, which is incorporated in the company's articles of association by virtue of article [1] of those articles] we, the undersigned, being all the members of the company who, at the date of this resolution would be entitled to attend and vote at general meetings of the company, hereby unanimously resolve upon the following resolution and agree that it shall be as valid and effective as if it had been passed as an elective resolution at a general meeting of the company duly convened and held.

That the company elects that the provisions of s.80A of the Companies Act 1985 shall apply in relation to any giving or renewal after the passing of this resolution of an authority to allot shares pursuant to section 80 of that Act.[1]

Dated

_____

_____

_____

[1]*File this resolution with Companies House.*

Company Number: _____

THE COMPANIES ACT 1985
PRIVATE COMPANY LIMITED BY SHARES
WRITTEN RESOLUTION

OF

_____ LIMITED

passed on _____

In accordance with [section 381A of the Companies Act 1985]/[article _____ of the company's articles of association]/[regulation 53 of Table A, which is incorporated in the company's articles of association by virtue of article [1] of those articles] we, the undersigned, being all the members of the company who, at the date of this resolution would be entitled to attend and vote at general meetings of the company, hereby unanimously resolve upon the following resolution and agree that it shall be as valid and effective as if it had been passed as an elective resolution at a general meeting of the company duly convened and held.

That in accordance with section 252 of the Companies Act 1985 the company hereby elects to dispense with the requirement of laying accounts and reports before the company in general meeting.[1]

Dated

_____

_____

_____

[1]File this resolution with Companies House. Accounts must still be prepared and sent out to members each year.

Form E21

Company Number: _____

THE COMPANIES ACT 1985
PRIVATE COMPANY LIMITED BY SHARES
WRITTEN RESOLUTION

OF

_____ **LIMITED**

passed on _____

In accordance with [section 381A of the Companies Act 1985]/[article _____ of the company's articles of association]/[regulation 53 of Table A, which is incorporated in the company's articles of association by virtue of article [1] of those articles] we, the undersigned, being all the members of the company who, at the date of this resolution would be entitled to attend and vote at general meetings of the company, hereby unanimously resolve upon the following resolution and agree that it shall be as valid and effective as if it had been passed as an elective resolution at a general meeting of the company duly convened and held.

That in accordance with section 366A of the Companies Act 1985 the company hereby elects to dispense with the requirement to hold annual general meetings.[1]

Dated

_____

_____

_____

[1]*File this resolution with Companies House. Any member can still ask for an AGM.*

Company Number: _____

THE COMPANIES ACT 1985
PRIVATE COMPANY LIMITED BY SHARES
WRITTEN RESOLUTION

OF

_____ LIMITED

passed on _____

In accordance with [section 381A of the Companies Act 1985]/[article _____ of the company's articles of association]/[regulation 53 of Table A, which is incorporated in the company's articles of association by virtue of article [1] of those articles] we, the undersigned, being all the members of the company who, at the date of this resolution would be entitled to attend and vote at general meetings of the company, hereby unanimously resolve upon the following resolution and agree that it shall be as valid and effective as if it had been passed as an elective resolution at a general meeting of the company duly convened and held.

That in accordance with section 386 of the Companies Act 1985 the company hereby elects to dispense with the obligation to appoint auditors annually.[1]

Dated

_____

_____

_____

[1]*File this resolution with Companies House.*

Company Number: _____

THE COMPANIES ACT 1985
PRIVATE COMPANY LIMITED BY SHARES
WRITTEN RESOLUTION

OF

_____ LIMITED

passed on _____

In accordance with [section 381A of the Companies Act 1985]/[article _____ of the Company's articles of association]/[regulation 53 of Table A, which is incorporated in the Company's articles of association by virtue of article [1] of those articles] we, the undersigned, being all the members of the Company who, at the date of this resolution would be entitled to attend and vote at general meetings of the Company, hereby unanimously resolve upon the following resolution and agree that it shall be as valid and effective as if it had been passed as an elective resolution at a general meeting of the company duly convened and held.

That in accordance with sections 369(4) and 378(3) of the Companies Act 1985 the Company hereby elects that the said provisions shall have effect as if for the reference to 95 per cent were substituted a reference to _____ per cent.[1]

Dated

_____

_____

_____

[1] *This percentage cannot be reduced lower than 90%. File this resolution with Companies House.*

Company Number: _____

THE COMPANIES ACT 1985
PRIVATE COMPANY LIMITED BY SHARES
WRITTEN RESOLUTION

OF

_____ LIMITED

passed on _____

In accordance with [section 381A of the Companies Act 1985]/[article _____ of the company's articles of association]/[regulation 53 of Table A, which is incorporated in the company's articles of association by virtue of article [1] of those articles] we, the undersigned, being all the members of the company who, at the date of this resolution would be entitled to attend and vote at general meetings of the company, hereby unanimously resolve upon the following resolution and agree that it shall be as valid and effective as if it had been passed as an ordinary resolution at a general meeting of the company duly convened and held.

THAT That in accordance with section 379A of the Companies Act 1985 the company hereby revokes the elective resolution of the company made on _____ whereby the company elected that the provisions of section 80A of the Companies Act 1985 should apply in relation to the authority to allot shares.[1]

Dated

_____

_____

_____

---

[1] File this resolution with Companies House.

Form E25

Company Number: _____

THE COMPANIES ACT 1985
PRIVATE COMPANY LIMITED BY SHARES
WRITTEN RESOLUTION

OF

_____ LIMITED

passed on _____

In accordance with [section 381A of the Companies Act 1985]/[article _____ of the company's articles of association]/[regulation 53 of Table A, which is incorporated in the company's articles of association by virtue of article [1] of those articles] we, the undersigned, being all the members of the company who, at the date of this resolution would be entitled to attend and vote at general meetings of the company, hereby unanimously resolve upon the following resolution and agree that it shall be as valid and effective as if it had been passed as an ordinary resolution at a general meeting of the company duly convened and held.

THAT That in accordance with section 379A of the Companies Act 1985 the company hereby revokes the elective resolution of the company made on _____ whereby the company dispensed with the laying of accounts and reports before the company in general meeting.[1]

Dated

_____

_____

_____

[1] File this resolution with Companies House.

Company Number: _____

THE COMPANIES ACT 1985
PRIVATE COMPANY LIMITED BY SHARES
WRITTEN RESOLUTION

OF

_____ **LIMITED**

passed on _____

In accordance with [section 381A of the Companies Act 1985]/[article _____ of the company's articles of association]/[regulation 53 of Table A, which is incorporated in the company's articles of association by virtue of article [1] of those articles] we, the undersigned, being all the members of the company who, at the date of this resolution would be entitled to attend and vote at general meetings of the company, hereby unanimously resolve upon the following resolution and agree that it shall be as valid and effective as if it had been passed as an ordinary resolution at a general meeting of the company duly convened and held.

That in accordance with section 379A of the Companies Act 1985 the company hereby revokes the elective resolution of the company made on _____ whereby the company dispenses with the holding of annual general meetings.[1]

Dated

_____

_____

_____

[1] File this resolution with Companies House.

Company Number: _____

THE COMPANIES ACT 1985
PRIVATE COMPANY LIMITED BY SHARES
WRITTEN RESOLUTION

OF

_____ LIMITED

passed on _____

In accordance with [section 381A of the Companies Act 1985]/[article _____ of the company's articles of association]/[regulation 53 of Table A, which is incorporated in the company's articles of association by virtue of article [1] of those articles] we, the undersigned, being all the members of the company who, at the date of this resolution would be entitled to attend and vote at general meetings of the company, hereby unanimously resolve upon the following resolution and agree that it shall be as valid and effective as if it had been passed as an ordinary resolution at a general meeting of the company duly convened and held.

That in accordance with section 379A of the Companies Act 1985 the company hereby revokes the elective resolution of the company made on _____ whereby the company dispensed with the annual appointment of auditors.[1]

Dated

_____

_____

_____

---

[1] File this resolution with Companies House.

Company Number: _____

THE COMPANIES ACT 1985
PRIVATE COMPANY LIMITED BY SHARES
WRITTEN RESOLUTION

OF

_____ LIMITED

passed on _____

In accordance with [section 381A of the Companies Act 1985]/[article _____ of the company's articles of association]/[regulation 53 of Table A, which is incorporated in the company's articles of association by virtue of article [1] of those articles] we, the undersigned, being all the members of the company who, at the date of this resolution would be entitled to attend and vote at general meetings of the company, hereby unanimously resolve upon the following resolution and agree that it shall be as valid and effective as if it had been passed as an ordinary resolution at a general meeting of the company duly convened and held.

That in accordance with section 379A of the Companies Act 1985 the company hereby revokes the elective resolution of the company made on _____ whereby the company elected to reduce the majority required to sanction short notice of general meetings.[1]

Dated

_____

_____

_____

[1] File this resolution with Companies House.

Form E29

Company Number: _____

THE COMPANIES ACT 1985
PRIVATE COMPANY LIMITED BY SHARES
WRITTEN RESOLUTION

OF

_____ LIMITED

passed on _____

In accordance with [section 381A of the Companies Act 1985]/[article
_____ of the company's articles of association]/[regulation 53
of Table A, which is incorporated in the company's articles of association
by virtue of article [1] of those articles] we, the undersigned, being all
the members of the company who, at the date of this resolution would
be entitled to attend and vote at general meetings of the company, hereby unanimously resolve upon the following resolution and agree that it
shall be as valid and effective as if it had been passed as a special resolution at a general meeting of the company duly convened and held.

That the company be re-registered as a public company as defined in section 1(3) of the Companies Act 1985.[1]

Dated

_____

_____

_____

[1]Send to the Companies House: copy of resolution, application to re-register, new memorandum and articles
of association, copy of latest balance sheet, auditors' report and statutory declaration from director or secretary (for more details, see footnote to Form C48).

Company Number: _____

THE COMPANIES ACT 1985
PRIVATE COMPANY LIMITED BY SHARES
WRITTEN RESOLUTION

OF

_____ LIMITED

passed on _____

In accordance with [section 381A of the Companies Act 1985]/[article _____ of the company's articles of association]/[regulation 53 of Table A, which is incorporated in the company's articles of association by virtue of article [1] of those articles] we, the undersigned, being all the members of the company who, at the date of this resolution would be entitled to attend and vote at general meetings of the company, hereby unanimously resolve upon the following resolution and agree that it shall be as valid and effective as if it had been passed as a special resolution at a general meeting of the company duly convened and held.

That the name of the company be changed to _____ with effect from _____.[1]

Dated

_____

_____

_____

[1]*File resolution with Companies House. Also send amended memorandum and articles and fee.*

Company Number: _____

THE COMPANIES ACT 1985
PRIVATE COMPANY LIMITED BY SHARES
WRITTEN RESOLUTION

OF

_____ LIMITED

passed on _____

In accordance with [section 381A of the Companies Act 1985]/[article _____ of the company's articles of association]/[regulation 53 of Table A, which is incorporated in the company's articles of association by virtue of article [1] of those articles] we, the undersigned, being all the members of the company who, at the date of this resolution would be entitled to attend and vote at general meetings of the company, hereby unanimously resolve upon the following resolution and agree that it shall be as valid and effective as if it had been passed as a special resolution at a general meeting of the company duly convened and held.

That the articles of association of the company be altered as follows:

(1) By the deletion of articles _____ and _____ and altering the subsequent numbering accordingly.

(2) By the addition of the new articles as set out in the attached document to be numbered _____ and _____ .

Dated

_____

_____

_____

Company Number: _____

THE COMPANIES ACT 1985
PRIVATE COMPANY LIMITED BY SHARES
WRITTEN RESOLUTION

OF

_____ LIMITED

passed on _____

In accordance with [section 381A of the Companies Act 1985]/[article _____ of the company's articles of association]/[regulation 53 of Table A, which is incorporated in the company's articles of association by virtue of article [1] of those articles] we, the undersigned, being all the members of the company who, at the date of this resolution would be entitled to attend and vote at general meetings of the company, hereby unanimously resolve upon the following resolution and agree that it shall be as valid and effective as if it had been passed as a special resolution at a general meeting of the company duly convened and held.

That the document attached to this resolution be approved and adopted as the new articles of association of the company to the exclusion of its existing articles.[1]

Dated

_____

_____

_____

[1]File new articles and special resolution with Companies House.

Form E33

Company Number: _____

THE COMPANIES ACT 1985
PRIVATE COMPANY LIMITED BY SHARES
WRITTEN RESOLUTION

OF

_____ LIMITED

passed on _____

In accordance with [section 381A of the Companies Act 1985]/[article _____ of the company's articles of association]/[regulation 53 of Table A, which is incorporated in the company's articles of association by virtue of article [1] of those articles] we, the undersigned, being all the members of the company who, at the date of this resolution would be entitled to attend and vote at general meetings of the company, hereby unanimously resolve upon the following resolution and agree that it shall be as valid and effective as if it had been passed as a special resolution at a general meeting of the company duly convened and held.

That the objects as set out in the document attached to this resolution be approved and adopted as the objects of the company in place of all existing objects and the company's memorandum of association be altered accordingly.[1]

Dated

_____

_____

_____

[1]*File amended memorandum and special resolution with Companies House.*

Company Number: _____

THE COMPANIES ACT 1985
PRIVATE COMPANY LIMITED BY SHARES
WRITTEN RESOLUTION

OF

_____ LIMITED

passed on _____

In accordance with [section 381A of the Companies Act 1985]/[article _____ of the company's articles of association]/[regulation 53 of Table A, which is incorporated in the company's articles of association by virtue of article [1] of those articles] we, the undersigned, being all the members of the company who, at the date of this resolution would be entitled to attend and vote at general meetings of the company, hereby unanimously resolve upon the following resolution and agree that it shall be as valid and effective as if it had been passed as an ordinary resolution at a general meeting of the company duly convened and held.

That a payment of £ _____ by the company to _____ in consideration for his retirement as director of the company be approved.

Dated

_____

_____

_____

Company Number: _____

THE COMPANIES ACT 1985
PRIVATE COMPANY LIMITED BY SHARES
WRITTEN RESOLUTION

OF

_____ LIMITED

passed on _____

In accordance with [section 381A of the Companies Act 1985]/[article _____ of the company's articles of association]/[regulation 53 of Table A, which is incorporated in the company's articles of association by virtue of article [1] of those articles] we, the undersigned, being all the members of the company who, at the date of this resolution would be entitled to attend and vote at general meetings of the company, hereby unanimously resolve upon the following resolution and agree that it shall be as valid and effective as if it had been passed as an ordinary resolution at a general meeting of the company duly convened and held.

That in accordance with section 319 of the Companies Act 1985 the members consent to the granting of a service contract to _____ which exceeds five years in duration on the terms set out in the document attached hereto.[1]

Dated

_____

_____

_____

[1]Contract must be sent to each member at or before the time at which the resolution is supplied to him for signature. If this resolution is to be proposed at a general meeting, contract must be available for inspection by members at the meeting and for fifteen days prior to the meeting at the registered office.

Company Number: _____

THE COMPANIES ACT 1985
PRIVATE COMPANY LIMITED BY SHARES
WRITTEN RESOLUTION

OF

_____ LIMITED

passed on _____

In accordance with [section 381A of the Companies Act 1985]/[article _____ of the company's articles of association]/[regulation 53 of Table A, which is incorporated in the company's articles of association by virtue of article [1] of those articles] we, the undersigned, being all the members of the company who, at the date of this resolution would be entitled to attend and vote at general meetings of the company, hereby unanimously resolve upon the following resolution and agree that it shall be as valid and effective as if it had been passed as an ordinary resolution at a general meeting of the company duly convened and held.

That all acts of the directors done prior to the date of this resolution be confirmed and ratified notwithstanding any matter that might otherwise cause their validity to be in doubt.[1]

Dated

_____

_____

_____

[1] This resolution ratifies any actions of the directors which are beyond the powers delegated to them in the company's articles. If the directors have acted beyond the powers of the company as set out in the objects clause in its memorandum of association, this resolution is not appropriate and legal advice should be sought.

Company Number: _____

THE COMPANIES ACT 1985
PRIVATE COMPANY LIMITED BY SHARES
WRITTEN RESOLUTION

OF

_____ LIMITED

passed on _____

In accordance with [section 381A of the Companies Act 1985]/[article _____ of the company's articles of association]/[regulation 53 of Table A, which is incorporated in the company's articles of association by virtue of article [1] of those articles] we, the undersigned, being all the members of the company who, at the date of this resolution would be entitled to attend and vote at general meetings of the company, hereby unanimously resolve upon the following resolution and agree that it shall be as valid and effective as if it had been passed as an ordinary resolution at a general meeting of the company duly convened and held.

That pursuant to regulation 96 of Table A (which is incorporated in the articles of association of the company by virtue of article _____ of these articles) _____, who is a director of this company, may vote on any resolution concerning a matter in which he has a personal interest notwithstanding article _____ of the company's articles of association.

Dated

_____

_____

_____

Company Number: _____

THE COMPANIES ACT 1985
PRIVATE COMPANY LIMITED BY SHARES
WRITTEN RESOLUTION

OF

_____ LIMITED

passed on _____

In accordance with [section 381A of the Companies Act 1985]/[article _____ of the company's articles of association]/[regulation 53 of Table A, which is incorporated in the company's articles of association by virtue of article [1] of those articles] we, the undersigned, being all the members of the company who, at the date of this resolution would be entitled to attend and vote at general meetings of the company, hereby unanimously resolve upon the following resolution and agree that it shall be as valid and effective as if it had been passed as an ordinary resolution at a general meeting of the company duly convened and held.

THAT the company's articles of association be altered by the insertion of the wording set out below as new article no._____ and the renumbering of the subsequent articles accordingly/in substitution for existing article no._____.[1]

The Directors shall not be required to retire by rotation and regulations 73 to 80 (inclusive) in Table A shall not apply to the Company.

Dated

_____

_____

_____

[1] Delete as appropriate. File resolution and copy of amended articles with Companies House.

Company Number: _____

THE COMPANIES ACT 1985
PRIVATE COMPANY LIMITED BY SHARES
WRITTEN RESOLUTION

OF

_____ **LIMITED**

passed on _____

In accordance with [section 381A of the Companies Act 1985]/[article _____ of the company's articles of association]/[regulation 53 of Table A, which is incorporated in the company's articles of association by virtue of article [1] of those articles] we, the undersigned, being all the members of the company who, at the date of this resolution would be entitled to attend and vote at general meetings of the company, hereby unanimously resolve upon the following resolution and agree that it shall be as valid and effective as if it had been passed as an ordinary resolution at a general meeting of the company duly convened and held.

THAT the company's articles of association be altered by the insertion of the wording set out below as new article no._____ and the renumbering of the subsequent articles accordingly/in substitution for existing article no._____.[1]

The Chairman shall not have a casting vote and regulation 50 in Table A shall not apply to the company.

Dated

_____

_____

_____

[1] Delete as appropriate. File resolution and copy of amended articles with Companies House.

Company Number: _____

THE COMPANIES ACT 1985
PRIVATE COMPANY LIMITED BY SHARES
WRITTEN RESOLUTION

OF

_____ LIMITED

passed on _____

In accordance with [section 381A of the Companies Act 1985]/[article _____ of the company's articles of association]/[regulation 53 of Table A, which is incorporated in the company's articles of association by virtue of article [1] of those articles] we, the undersigned, being all the members of the company who, at the date of this resolution would be entitled to attend and vote at general meetings of the company, hereby unanimously resolve upon the following resolution and agree that it shall be as valid and effective as if it had been passed as an ordinary resolution at a general meeting of the company duly convened and held.

THAT the company's articles of association be altered by the insertion of the wording set out below as new article no._____ and the renumbering of the subsequent articles accordingly/in substitution for existing article no._____.[1]

(a) A director may vote at any meeting of the directors or of any committee of the directors on any resolution notwithstanding that it in any way concerns or relates to a matter in which he has, directly or indirectly, any kind of interest whatsoever and if he shall vote on any such resolution as aforesaid his vote shall be counted and in relation to any such resolution as aforesaid he shall (whether or not he shall vote on the same) be taken into account in calculating the quorum present at the meeting.

(b) Regulations 94 to 97 (inclusive) in Table A shall not apply to the company.

Dated

_____

_____

_____

[1] *Delete as appropriate. File resolution and copy of amended articles with Companies House.*

Company Number: _____

THE COMPANIES ACT 1985
PRIVATE COMPANY LIMITED BY SHARES
WRITTEN RESOLUTION

OF

_____ LIMITED

passed on _____

In accordance with [section 381A of the Companies Act 1985]/[article _____ of the company's articles of association]/[regulation 53 of Table A, which is incorporated in the company's articles of association by virtue of article [1] of those articles] we, the undersigned, being all the members of the company who, at the date of this resolution would be entitled to attend and vote at general meetings of the company, hereby unanimously resolve upon the following resolution and agree that it shall be as valid and effective as if it had been passed as an ordinary resolution at a general meeting of the company duly convened and held.

THAT the company's articles of association be altered by the insertion of the wording set out below as new article no._____ and the renumbering of the subsequent articles accordingly/in substitution for existing article no._____.[1]

The directors may, in their absolute discretion and without assigning any reason, decline to register the transfer of a share, whether or not it is a fully paid share and regulation 24 in Table A shall not apply to the company.

Dated

_____

_____

_____

[1] Delete as appropriate. File resolution and copy of amended articles with Companies House.

Company Number: _____

THE COMPANIES ACT 1985
PRIVATE COMPANY LIMITED BY SHARES
WRITTEN RESOLUTION

OF

_____ LIMITED

passed on _____

In accordance with [section 381A of the Companies Act 1985]/[article _____ of the company's articles of association]/[regulation 53 of Table A, which is incorporated in the company's articles of association by virtue of article [1] of those articles] we, the undersigned, being all the members of the company who, at the date of this resolution would be entitled to attend and vote at general meetings of the company, hereby unanimously resolve upon the following resolution and agree that it shall be as valid and effective as if it had been passed as an ordinary resolution at a general meeting of the company duly convened and held.

THAT the company's articles of association be altered by the insertion of the wording set out below as new article no._____ and the renumbering of the subsequent articles accordingly/in substitution for existing article no._____.[1]

In accordance with section 91(1) of the Companies Act 1985, sections 89(1) and 90(1) to (6) (inclusive) shall not apply to the company.

Dated

_____

_____

_____

[1] Delete as appropriate. File resolution and copy of amended articles with Companies House.

Company Number: _____

THE COMPANIES ACT 1985
PRIVATE COMPANY LIMITED BY SHARES
WRITTEN RESOLUTION

OF

_____ LIMITED

passed on _____

In accordance with [section 381A of the Companies Act 1985]/[article _____ of the company's articles of association]/[regulation 53 of Table A, which is incorporated in the company's articles of association by virtue of article [1] of those articles] we, the undersigned, being all the members of the company who, at the date of this resolution would be entitled to attend and vote at general meetings of the company, hereby unanimously resolve upon the following resolution and agree that it shall be as valid and effective as if it had been passed as an ordinary resolution at a general meeting of the company duly convened and held.

THAT the company's articles of association be altered by the insertion of the wording set out below as new article no._____ and the renumbering of the subsequent articles accordingly/in substitution for existing article no._____.[1]

(a)   If a quorum is not present within half an hour from the time appointed for a general meeting the general meeting shall stand adjourned to the same day in the next week at the same time and place or to such other day and at such other time and place as the directors may determine and if at the adjourned general meeting a quorum is not present within half an hour from the time appointed such adjourned general meeting shall be dissolved.

(b)   Regulation 41 in Table A shall not apply to the company.

Dated

_____

_____

_____

---

[1] *Delete as appropriate. File resolution and copy of amended articles with Companies House.*

Company Number: _____

THE COMPANIES ACT 1985
PRIVATE COMPANY LIMITED BY SHARES
WRITTEN RESOLUTION

OF

_____ LIMITED

passed on _____

In accordance with [section 381A of the Companies Act 1985]/[article _____ of the company's articles of association]/[regulation 53 of Table A, which is incorporated in the company's articles of association by virtue of article [1] of those articles] we, the undersigned, being all the members of the company who, at the date of this resolution would be entitled to attend and vote at general meetings of the company, hereby unanimously resolve upon the following resolution and agree that it shall be as valid and effective as if it had been passed as an ordinary resolution at a general meeting of the company duly convened and held.

THAT the company's articles of association be altered by the insertion of the wording set out below as new article no._____ and the renumbering of the subsequent articles accordingly/in substitution for existing article no._____.[1]

(a) Regulation 64 in Table A does not apply to the company.

(b) The maximum number and minimum number respectively of the Directors may be determined from time to time by Ordinary Resolution in General Meeting of the company. Subject to and in default of any such determination there shall be no maximum number of Directors and the minimum number of Directors shall be one. Whensoever the minimum number of Directors shall be one, a sole Director shall have authority to exercise all the powers and discretions by Table A and by these articles expressed to be vested in the Directors generally and regulation 89 in Table A shall be modified accordingly.

Dated

_____

_____

_____

[1] Delete as appropriate. File resolution and copy of amended articles with Companies House.

Form E45

Company Number: _____

THE COMPANIES ACT 1985
PRIVATE COMPANY LIMITED BY SHARES
WRITTEN RESOLUTION

OF

_____ LIMITED

passed on _____

In accordance with [section 381A of the Companies Act 1985]/[article _____of the company's articles of association]/[regulation 53 of Table A, which is incorporated in the company's articles of association by virtue of article [1] of those articles] we, the undersigned, being all the members of the company who, at the date of this resolution would be entitled to attend and vote at general meetings of the company, hereby unanimously resolve upon the following resolution and agree that it shall be as valid and effective as if it had been passed as an ordinary resolution at a general meeting of the company duly convened and held.

THAT the company's articles of association be altered by the insertion of the wording set out below as new article no._____ and the renumbering of the subsequent articles accordingly/in substitution for existing article no._____.[1]

An alternate director shall not be entitled to receive any remuneration from the company, save that he may be paid by the company such part (if any) of the remuneration otherwise payable to his appointor as such appointor may by notice in writing to the company form time to time direct and the first sentence of regulation 66 in Table A shall be modified accordingly

Dated

_____

_____

_____

[1] Delete as appropriate. File resolution and copy of amended articles with Companies House.

Company Number: _____

THE COMPANIES ACT 1985
PRIVATE COMPANY LIMITED BY SHARES
WRITTEN RESOLUTION

OF

_____ LIMITED

passed on _____

In accordance with [section 381A of the Companies Act 1985]/[article _____ of the company's articles of association]/[regulation 53 of Table A, which is incorporated in the company's articles of association by virtue of article [1] of those articles] we, the undersigned, being all the members of the company who, at the date of this resolution would be entitled to attend and vote at general meetings of the company, hereby unanimously resolve upon the following resolution and agree that it shall be as valid and effective as if it had been passed as an ordinary resolution at a general meeting of the company duly convened and held.

That the company's articles of association be altered by the insertion of the wording set out below as new article no._____ and the renumbering of the subsequent articles accordingly/in substitution for existing article no._____.[1]

Every director for the time being of the company shall have the following rights:

(a) if at any General Meeting a resolution is proposed to remove him from office, he shall be entitled to demand a poll and on that poll he shall have when voting against such resolution ____[2] votes for each share of which he is the holder; and

(b) if at any General Meeting a poll is duly demanded on a resolution to delete or amend the provisions of this article, he shall be entitled to demand a poll and on that poll he shall have when voting against such resolution ____[3] votes for each share of which he is the holder.

and regulation 54 in Table A shall be modified accordingly.

Dated

_____

_____

_____

[1] Delete as appropriate. File resolution and copy of amended articles with Companies House.

Company Number: _____

THE COMPANIES ACT 1985
PRIVATE COMPANY LIMITED BY SHARES
WRITTEN RESOLUTION

OF

_____ LIMITED

passed on _____

In accordance with [section 381A of the Companies Act 1985]/[article _____ of the company's articles of association]/[regulation 53 of Table A, which is incorporated in the company's articles of association by virtue of article [1] of those articles] we, the undersigned, being all the members of the company who, at the date of this resolution would be entitled to attend and vote at general meetings of the company, hereby unanimously resolve upon the following resolution and agree that it shall be as valid and effective as if it had been passed as an ordinary resolution at a general meeting of the company duly convened and held.

THAT the company's articles of association be altered by the insertion of the wording set out below as new article no._____ and the renumbering of the subsequent articles accordingly/in substitution for existing article no._____.[1]

The directors are generally and unconditionally authorised for the purposes of section 80 of the Companies Act to exercise any powers of the company to allot and grant rights to subscribe for or convert securities into share of the company up to the amount of the authorised share capital with which the company is incorporated at any time or times during the period of the five years from the date of incorporation and the directors may after that period allot any shares or grant any such rights under this authority in pursuance of an offer or agreement so to do made by the company within that period. The authority hereby given may at any time (subject to section 80 of the Companies Act 1985) be renewed, revoked or varied by ordinary resolution of the company in general meeting.

Dated

_____

_____

_____

[1] Delete as appropriate. File resolution and copy of amended articles with Companies House.

Glossary

Accounting reference date — the annual anniversary upon which a company's financial year ends.

Accounting reference period — the period which ends on the accounting reference date.

Administration order — the order of a court to appoint an administrator to manage a company in financial difficulties in an attempt to secure its survival or winding-up.

Allotment — the appropriation of shares in the capital of the company to the applicants for those shares, by the board.

Annual General Meeting (AGM) — obligatory annual meetings of a company's shareholders to lay the annual accounts and directors' and auditors' reports before the shareholders and deal with other matters. Private companies can dispense with the need for AGMs by passing elective resolutions.

Annual Return — a prescribed form which must be filed annually with Companies House by a limited company, detailing the company's activities for the period up to the anniversary of the company's incorporation.

Articles of Association (or 'articles') — the document containing the company's regulations for its internal management.

Assets — anything owned with monetary value. This includes both real and personal property.

Auditor — a person appointed to examine the accounts of a registered company and to report on them to company members.

Authorised Capital — the nominal capital which the company is authorised to issue by its memorandum of association. This may be increased by an ordinary or special resolution depending on the provisions of the articles of association.

Board — the directors of a company.

Board Meeting — a meeting of the directors.

Company seal — a company may execute deeds by affixing its seal to them. There is no longer any requirement for a company to have seal and it may execute deeds by either two directors or a director and the company secretary signing the relevant document.

Director — an officer of the company who manages company business and has a duty of care, skill and good faith.

Elective Resolution — a resolution which a private company is entitled to pass to reduce or remove certain administrative or formal requirements. It requires the consent of all those shareholders entitled to vote.

Extraordinary General Meeting — any meeting of company members other than the annual general meeting.

Extraordinary Resolution — a resolution required to effect decisions in certain circumstances (e.g. a creditors' winding up) and which requires a majority of not less than 75% of the company members voting in person or by proxy at a general meeting.

General Meeting — a meeting of shareholders. It may be an annual general meeting or an Extraordinary General Meeting where shareholders give their approval for transactions.

Incorporate — to form a limited company by following procedures prescribed by law. On incorporation the limited company becomes a separate legal entity distinct from its owners.

Insolvency — the inability of a company to meet its debts as they become due.

Issued shares — shares which have been actually allotted by the company and in respect of which the allottees have been entered in the company's register of members.

Member — person whose name has been entered in the company's register of members in respect of the shares he holds in the company.

Memorandum of Association — the company's charter enabling the outsider to establish the extent of the company's powers.

Minutes — written records of formal proceedings of shareholders' and directors' meetings.

Ordinary Resolution — a decision reached by a simple majority (more than 50%) of company members voting in person or by proxy.

Poll — ascertaining the will of the shareholders at a general meeting of the company by counting shareholders' votes according to the size of their share holdings. On a poll a proxy may vote.

Pre-emption — the rights of existing shareholders granting them first option to acquire shares which are to be transferred or issued in proportion to their present share holding.

Proxy — authorisation by a shareholder allowing another to vote his shares.

Public Limited Company — a type of company incorporated by registration under the Companies Act which may offer its shares to the public (a private company cannot do this) and is subject to a number of additional requirements under the Companies Act.

Quorum — the number of shareholders or directors necessary for vote a valid meeting.

Registered office — the postal address of the company notified to Companies House.

Remuneration — payment for services.

Resolution — decision made by directors or shareholders in accordance with requisite majorities set out in articles of association. Resolutions may be approved in meetings or by written resolution.

Share certificate — written and executed instrument showing who holds title to a particular share or series of shares.

Service business — a business that sells service or advice instead of a tangible product.

Shareholder — a holder of one or more shares in the capital of a company.

Special Resolution — a decision reached by not less than 75 per cent of company members voting in person or by proxy at a general meeting.

Statutory Books — the records that a company must keep as required by law. Changes must in many cases be notified to Companies House. The records should be kept at the company's registered office and are available to the public for inspection.

Subscriber — a person who signs the memorandum of association and is issued the first shares in a new company.

Table A — regulations for the management of a company from the Schedule to Statutory Instrument 1985/805 which are commonly adopted as the articles of association of companies (see page 157).

Written Resolution — a resolution passed either by the shareholders or the directors of the company by signing a written form of the resolution rather than voting at a meeting of the company or at a meeting of the directors of the company.

Register of   Members

Name Alexander Palmer
Address 85 Preston Square
London: SW6 5CN
Date of entry as shareholder 4-1-97 **Date of cessation of membership** _____

| Date of Allotment OR Entry of Transfer | References in Register | | Number of shares | No. of Share Certificate | Amount paid or agreed to be considered as paid | Acquisitions |
	Allotments	Transfers				
11-1-97	✓		1	1	£1	

Dividends to Alexander Palmer

Class of Share Ordinary   **Denomination** £1 each

Disposals	Balance	Remarks
	£1	

Name Julia Etheridge
Address 16 St. George's Crescent
Reading RG7 9XY
Date of entry as shareholder 4-1-97 **Date of cessation of membership** _____

| Date of Allotment OR Entry of Transfer | References in Register | | Number of shares | No. of Share Certificate | Amount paid or agreed to be considered as paid | Acquisitions |
	Allotments	Transfers				
11-1-97	✓		1	2	£1	

Dividends to Julia Etheridge

Class of Share Ordinary   **Denomination** £1 each

Disposals	Balance	Remarks
	£1	

Register of   Directors

Surname (or Corporate Name) Palmer
Forenames(s) Alexander
any former Forenames or Surnames _____

Nationality British **Date of Birth** 3-2-55
Residential Address (or Registered or Principal Office) 85 Preston Square
London SW6 5CN

Other Directorships None	Date of Resignation

Business Occupation Company Director
Date of Appointment 3-1-97 minute 11-1-97
Date of filing particulars 3-1-97
Date of Resignation or Cessation _____ minute _____
Date of filing particulars

Surname (or Corporate Name) Etheridge
Forenames(s) Julia
any former Forenames or Surnames _____

Nationality British **Date of Birth** 29-9-57
Residential Address (or Registered or Principal Office) 16 St. George's Crescent
Reading RG7 9XY

Other Directorships WA Limited	Date of Resignation

Business Occupation Sales Executive
Date of Appointment 3-1-97 minute 11-1-97
Date of filing particulars 3-1-97
Date of Resignation or Cessation _____ minute _____
Date of filing particulars

Surname (or Corporate Name) _____
Forenames(s) _____
any former Forenames or Surnames _____

Nationality _____ **Date of Birth** _____
Residential Address (or Registered or Principal Office) _____

Other Directorships	Date of Resignation

Business Occupation _____
Date of Appointment _____ minute _____
Date of filing particulars _____
Date of Resignation or Cessation _____ minute _____
Date of filing particulars _____

Register of   Secretaries

| Surname (or Corporate Name) Palmer |
| Forenames(s) Alexander |
| any former Forenames or Surnames |
| Date of Appointment   3-1-97   minute 11-1-97 |
| Date of filing particulars |

| Residential Address (or Registered or Principal Office) 85 Preston Square |
| London SW6 5CN |
| Date of Resignation or Cessation_____minute _____ |
| Date of filing particulars |

| Surname (or Corporate Name) |
| Forenames(s) |
| any former Forenames or Surnames |
| Date of Appointment _____ minute _____ |
| Date of filing particulars |

| Residential Address (or Registered or Principal Office) |
| Date of Resignation or Cessation_____minute _____ |
| Date of filing particulars |

| Surname (or Corporate Name) |
| Forenames(s) |
| any former Forenames or Surnames |
| Date of Appointment _____ minute _____ |
| Date of filing particulars |

| Residential Address (or Registered or Principal Office) |
| Date of Resignation or Cessation_____minute _____ |
| Date of filing particulars |

| Surname (or Corporate Name) |
| Forenames(s) |
| any former Forenames or Surnames |
| Date of Appointment _____ minute _____ |
| Date of filing particulars |

| Residential Address (or Registered or Principal Office) |
| Date of Resignation or Cessation_____minute _____ |
| Date of filing particulars |

| Surname (or Corporate Name) |
| Forenames(s) |
| any former Forenames or Surnames |
| Date of Appointment _____ minute _____ |
| Date of filing particulars |

| Residential Address (or Registered or Principal Office) |
| Date of Resignation or Cessation_____minute _____ |
| Date of filing particulars |

Register of   Directors' Interests

Name and Address of Person Interested Alexander Palmer
85 Preston Square, London SW6 5CN

Classes of Share Capital or Debentures Ordinary shares
(a) 1 share of £1 each.
(b)

| Entry | | Date of | | Nature of Event |
No.	Date	Event	Notification	
1	4-1-97	3-1-97	4-1-97	Subscriber to Memorandum of Association

| No. of shares involved | | No. of Shares in which interested after event | Price consideration | Remarks |
Acquisitions	Disposals			
1		1	£1	

Name and Address of Person Interested Julia Etheridge
16 St. George's Crescent, Reading RG7 9XY

Classes of Share Capital or Debentures Ordinary shares
(a) 1 share of £1 each.
(b)

| Entry | | Date of | | Nature of Event |
No.	Date	Event	Notification	
2	4-1-97	3-1-97	4-1-97	Subscriber to Memorandum of Association

| No. of shares involved | | No. of Shares in which interested after event | Price consideration | Remarks |
Acquisitions	Disposals			
1		1	£1	

COMPANIES ACT 1985 TABLE A
(SI 1985/805, SCHEDULE)
REGULATIONS FOR MANAGEMENT OF A
COMPANY LIMITED BY SHARES

Interpretation

1. In these regulations -

    (a) 'the Act' means the Companies Act 1985 including any statutory modification or re-enactment thereof for the time being in force.

    (b) 'the articles' means the articles of the company.

    (c) 'clear days' in relation to the period of a notice means that period excluding the day when the notice is given or deemed to be given and the day for which it is given or on which it is to take effect.

    (d) 'executed' includes any mode of execution.

    (e) 'office' means the registered office of the company.

    (g) 'the holder' in relation to shares means the member whose name is entered in the register of members as the holder of the shares.

    (h) 'the seal' means the common seal of the company.

    (i) 'secretary' means the secretary of the company or any other person appointed to perform the duties of the secretary of the company, including a joint, assistant or deputy secretary.

    (j) 'the United Kingdom' means Great Britain and Northern Ireland.

    (k) unless the context otherwise requires, words or expressions contained in these regulations bear the same meaning as in the Act but excluding any statutory modification thereof not in force when these regulations become binding on the company.

Share capital

2. Subject to the provisions of the Act and without prejudice to any rights attached to any existing shares, any share may be issued with such rights or restrictions as the company may by ordinary resolution determine.

3. Subject to the provisions of the Act, shares may be issued which are to be redeemed or are to be liable to be redeemed at the option of the company or the holder on such terms and in such manner as may be provided by the articles.

4. The company may exercise the powers of paying commissions conferred by the Act. Subject to the provisions of the Act, any such commission may be satisfied by the payment of cash or by the allotment of fully or partly paid shares or partly in one way and partly in the other.

5. Except as required by law, no person shall be recognised by the company as hold-

ing any share upon any trust and (except as otherwise provided by the articles or by law) the company shall not be bound by or recognise any interest in any share except an absolute right to the entirety thereof in the holder.

Share certificates

6. Every member, upon becoming the holder of any shares, shall be entitled without payment to one certificate for all the shares of each class held by him (and, upon transferring a part of his holding of shares of any class, to a certificate for the balance of such holding) or several certificates each for one or more of his shares upon payment for every certificate after the first of such reasonable sum as the directors may determine. Every certificate shall be sealed with the seal and shall specify the number, class and distinguishing numbers (if any) of the shares to which it relates and the amount or respective amounts paid up thereon. The company shall not be bound to issue more than one certificate for shares held jointly by several persons and delivery of a certificate to one joint holder shall be a sufficient delivery to all of them.

7. If a share certificate is defaced, worn-out, lost or destroyed, it may be renewed on such terms (if any) as to evidence and indemnity and payment of the expenses reasonably incurred by the company in investigating evidence as the directors may determine but otherwise free of charge, and (in the case of defacement or wearing-out) on delivery up of the old certificate.

Lien

8. The company shall have a first and paramount lien on every share (not being a fully paid share) for all moneys (whether presently payable or not) payable at a fixed time or called in respect of that share. The directors may at any time declare any share to be wholly or in part exempt from the provisions of this regulation. The company's lien on a share shall extend to any amount payable in respect of it.

9. The company may sell in such manner as the directors determine any shares on which the company has a lien if a sum in respect of which the lien exists is presently payable and is not paid within fourteen clear days after notice has been given to the holder of the share or to the person entitled to it in consequence of the death or bankruptcy of the holder, demanding payment and stating that if the notice is not complied with the shares may be sold.

10. To give effect to a sale the directors may authorise some person to execute an instrument of transfer of the shares sold to, or in accordance with the directions of, the purchaser. The title of the transferee to the shares shall not be affected by any irregularity in or invalidity of the proceedings in reference to the sale.

11. The net proceeds of the sale, after payment of the costs, shall be applied in payment of so much of the sum for which the lien exists as is presently payable, and any residue shall (upon surrender to the company for cancellation of the certificate for the shares sold and subject to a like lien for any moneys not presently payable as existed upon the shares before the sale) be paid to the person entitled to the shares at the date of the sale.

Calls on shares and forfeiture

12. Subject to the terms of allotment, the directors may make calls upon the members in respect of any moneys unpaid on their shares (whether in respect of nominal value or premium) and each member shall (subject to receiving at least fourteen clear days' notice specifying when and where payment is to be made) pay to the company as required by the notice the amount called on his shares. A call may be required to be paid by instalments. A call may, before receipt by the company of any sum due thereunder, be revoked in whole or part and payment of a call may be postponed in whole or part. A person upon whom a call is made shall remain liable for calls made upon him notwithstanding the subsequent transfer of the shares in respect whereof the call was made.

13. A call shall be deemed to have been made at the time when the resolution of the directors authorising the call was passed.

14. The joint holders of a share shall be jointly and severally liable to pay all calls in respect thereof.

15. If a call remains unpaid after it has become due and payable the person from whom it is due and payable shall pay interest on the amount unpaid from the day it became due and payable until it is paid at the rate fixed by the terms of allotment of the share or in the notice of the call or, if no rate is fixed, at the appropriate rate (as defined by the Act) but the directors may waive payment of the interest wholly or in part.

16. An amount payable in respect of a share on allotment or at any fixed date, whether in respect of nominal value or premium or as an instalment of a call, shall be deemed to be a call and if it is not paid the provisions of the articles shall apply as if that amount had become due and payable by virtue of a call.

17. Subject to the terms of allotment, the directors may make arrangements on the issue of shares for a difference between the holders in the amounts and times of payment of calls on their shares.

18. If a call remains unpaid after it has become due and payable the directors may give to the person from whom it is due not less than 14 clear days' notice requiring payment of the amount unpaid together with any interest which may have accrued. The notice shall name the place where payment is to be made and shall state that if the notice is not complied with the shares in respect of which the call was made will be liable to be forfeited.

19. If the notice is not complied with any share in respect of which it was given may, before the payment required by the notice has been made, be forfeited by a resolution of the directors and the forfeiture shall include all dividends or other moneys payable in respect of the forfeited shares and not paid before the forfeiture.

20. Subject to the provisions of the Act, a forfeited share may be sold, re-allotted or otherwise disposed of on such terms and in such manner as the directors determine either to the person who was before the forfeiture the holder or to any other person and at any time before sale, re-allotment or other disposition, the forfeiture may be cancelled on such terms as the directors think fit. Where for the purposes of its disposal a forfeited share is to be transferred to any person the directors may authorise some person to execute an instrument of transfer of the share to that person.

21. A person any of whose shares have been forfeited shall cease to be a member in

respect of them and shall surrender to the company for cancellation the certificate for the shares forfeited but shall remain liable to the company for all moneys which at the date of forfeiture were presently payable by him to the company in respect of those shares with interest at the rate at which interest was payable on those moneys before the forfeiture or, if no interest was so payable, at the appropriate rate (as defined in the Act) from the date of forfeiture until payment but the directors may waive payment wholly or in part or enforce payment without any allowance for the value of the shares at the time of forfeiture or for any consideration received on their disposal.

22. A statutory declaration by a director or the secretary that a share has been forfeited on a specified date shall be conclusive evidence of the facts stated in it as against all persons claiming to be entitled to the share and the declaration shall (subject to the execution of an instrument of transfer if necessary) constitute a good title to the share and the person to whom the share is disposed of shall not be bound to see to the application of the consideration, if any, nor shall his title to the share be affected by any irregularity in or invalidity of the proceedings in reference to the forfeiture or disposal of the share.

Transfer of shares

23. The instrument of transfer of a share may be in any usual form or in any other form which the directors may approve and shall be executed by or on behalf of the transferor and, unless the share is fully paid, by or on behalf of the transferee.

24. The directors may refuse to register the transfer of a share which is not fully paid to a person of whom they do not approve and they may refuse to register the transfer of a share on which the company has a lien. They may also refuse to register a transfer unless

    (a) it is lodged at the office or at such other place as the directors may appoint and is accompanied by the certificate for the shares to which it relates and such other evidence as the directors may reasonably require to show the right of the transferor to make the transfer;

    (b) it is in respect of only one class of shares; and

    (c) it is in favour of not more than four transferees.

25. If the directors refuse to register a transfer of a share, they shall within two months after the date on which the transfer was lodged with the company send to the transferee notice of the refusal.

26. The registration of transfers of shares or of transfers of any class of shares may be suspended at such times and for such periods (not exceeding thirty days in any year) as the directors may determine.

27. No fee shall be charged for the registration of any instrument of transfer or other document relating to or affecting the title to any share.

28. The company shall be entitled to retain any instrument of transfer which is registered, but any instrument of transfer which the directors refuse to register shall be returned to the person lodging it when notice of the refusal is given.

Transmission of shares

29. If a member dies the survivor or survivors where he was a joint holder, and his personal representatives where he was a sole holder or the only survivor of joint holders, shall be the only persons recognised by the company as having any title to his interest; but nothing herein contained shall release the estate of a deceased member from any liability in respect of any share which had been jointly held by him.

30. A person becoming entitled to a share in consequence of the death or bankruptcy of a member may, upon such evidence being produced as the directors may properly require, elect either to become the holder of the share or to have some person nominated by him registered as the transferee. If he elects to become the holder he shall give notice to the company to that effect. If he elects to have another person registered he shall execute an instrument of transfer of the share to that person. All the articles relating to the transfer of shares shall apply to the notice or instrument of transfer as if it were an instrument of transfer executed by the member and the death or bankruptcy of the member had not occurred.

31. A person becoming entitled to a share in consequence of the death or bankruptcy of a member shall have the rights to which he would be entitled if he were the holder of the share, except that he shall not, before being registered as the holder of the share, be entitled in respect of it to attend or vote at any meeting of the company or at any separate meeting of the holders of any class of shares in the company.

Alteration of share capital

32. The company may by ordinary resolution -

   (a) increase its share capital by new shares of such amount as the resolution prescribes;

   (b) consolidate and divide all or any of its share capital into shares of larger amount than its existing shares;

   (c) subject to the provisions of the Act, sub-divide its shares, or any of them, into shares of smaller amount and the resolution may determine that, as between the shares resulting from the sub-division, any of them may have any preference or advantage as compared with the others; and

   (d) cancel shares which, at the date of the passing of the resolution, have not been taken or agreed to be taken by any person and diminish the amount of its share capital by the amount of the shares so cancelled.

33. Whenever as a result of a consolidation of shares any members would become entitled to fractions of a share, the directors may, on behalf of those members, sell the shares representing the fractions for the best price reasonably obtainable to any person (including, subject to the provisions of the Act, the company) and distribute the net proceeds of sale in due proportion among those members, and the directors may authorise some person to execute an instrument of transfer of the shares to, or in accordance with the directions of, the purchaser. The transferee shall not be bound to see to the application of the purchase money nor shall his title to the shares be affected by any irregularity in or invalidity of the proceedings in reference to the sale.

34. Subject to the provisions of the Act, the company may by special resolution reduce its share capital, any capital redemption reserve and any share premium account in any way.

Purchase of own shares

35. Subject to the provisions of the Act, the company may purchase its own shares (including any redeemable shares) and, if it is a private company, make a payment in respect of the redemption or purchase of its own shares otherwise than out of distributable profits of the company or the proceeds of a fresh issue of shares.

General meetings

36. All general meetings other than annual general meetings shall be called extraordinary general meetings.

37. The directors may call general meetings and, on the requisition of members pursuant to the provisions of the Act, shall forthwith proceed to convene an extraordinary general meeting for a date not later than eight weeks after receipt of the requisition. If there are not within the United Kingdom sufficient directors to call a general meeting, any director or any member of the company may call a general meeting.

Notice of general meetings

38. An annual general meeting and an extraordinary general meeting called for the passing of a special resolution or a resolution appointing a person as a director shall be called by at least twenty-one clear days' notice. All other extraordinary general meetings shall be called by at least fourteen clear days' notice but a general meeting may be called by shorter notice if it is so agreed -

    (a) in the case of an annual general meeting, by all the members entitled to attend and vote thereat; and

    (b) in the case of any other meeting by a majority in number of the members having a right to attend and vote being a majority together holding not less than ninety-five per cent. in nominal value of the shares giving that right.

    The notice shall specify the time and place of the meeting and the general nature of the business to be transacted and, in the case of an annual general meeting, shall specify the meeting as such.

    Subject to the provisions of the articles and to any restrictions imposed on any shares, the notice shall be given to all the members, to all persons entitled to a share in consequence of the death or bankruptcy of a member and to the directors and auditors.

39. The accidental omission to give notice of a meeting to, or the non-receipt of notice of a meeting by, any person entitled to receive notice shall not invalidate the proceedings at that meeting.

Proceedings at general meetings

40. No business shall be transacted at any meeting unless a quorum is present. Two persons entitled to vote upon the business to be transacted, each being a member or a proxy for a member or a duly authorised representative of a corporation, shall be a quorum.

41. If such a quorum is not present within half an hour from the time appointed for the meeting, or if during a meeting such a quorum ceases to be present, the meeting shall stand adjourned to the same day in the next week at the same time and place or to such time and place as the directors may determine.

42. The chairman, if any, of the board of directors or in his absence some other director nominated by the directors shall preside as chairman of the meeting, but if neither the chairman nor such other director (if any) be present within fifteen minutes after the time appointed for holding the meeting and willing to act, the directors present shall elect one of their number to be chairman and, if there is only one director present and willing to act, he shall be chairman.

43. If no director is willing to act as chairman, or if no director is present within fifteen minutes after the time appointed for holding the meeting, the members present and entitled to vote shall choose one of their number to be chairman.

44. A director shall, notwithstanding that he is not a member, be entitled to attend and speak at any general meeting and at any separate meeting of the holders of any class of shares in the company.

45. The chairman may, with the consent of a meeting at which a quorum is present (and shall if so directed by the meeting), adjourn the meeting from time to time and from place to place, but no business shall be transacted at an adjourned meeting other than business which might properly have been transacted at the meeting had the adjournment not taken place. When a meeting is adjourned for fourteen days or more, at least seven clear days' notice shall be given specifying the time and place of the adjourned meeting and the general nature of the business to be transacted. Otherwise it shall not be necessary to give any such notice.

46. A resolution put to the vote of a meeting shall be decided on a show of hands unless before, or on the declaration of the result of, the show of hands a poll is duly demanded. Subject to the provisions of the Act, a poll may be demanded-

    (a) by the chairman; or

    (b) by at least two members having the right to vote at the meeting; or

    (c) by a member or members representing not less than one-tenth of the total voting rights of all the members having the right to vote at the meeting; or

    (d) by a member or members holding shares conferring a right to vote at the meeting being shares on which an aggregate sum has been paid up equal to not less than one-tenth of the total sum paid up on all the shares conferring that right; and a demand by a person as proxy for a member shall be the same as a demand by the member.

47. Unless a poll is duly demanded a declaration by the chairman that a resolution has been carried or carried unanimously, or by a particular majority, or lost, or not carried by a particular majority and an entry to that effect in the minutes of the meeting shall be conclusive evidence of the fact without proof of the number or

proportion of the votes recorded in favour of or against the resolution.

48. The demand for a poll may, before the poll is taken, be withdrawn but only with the consent of the chairman and a demand so withdrawn shall not be taken to have invalidated the result of a show of hands declared before the demand was made.

49. A poll shall be taken as the chairman directs and he may appoint scrutineers (who need not be members) and fix a time and place for declaring the result of the poll. The result of the poll shall be deemed to be the resolution of the meeting at which the poll was demanded.

50. In the case of an equality of votes, whether on a show of hands or on a poll, the chairman shall be entitled to a casting vote in addition to any other vote he may have.

51. A poll demanded on the election of a chairman or on a question of adjournment shall be taken forthwith. A poll demanded on any other question shall be taken either forthwith or at such time and place as the chairman directs not being more than thirty days after the poll is demanded. The demand for a poll shall not prevent the continuance of a meeting for the transaction of any business other than the question on which the poll was demanded. If a poll is demanded before the declaration of the result of a show of hands and the demand is duly withdrawn, the meeting shall continue as if the demand had not been made.

52. No notice need be given of a poll not taken forthwith if the time and place at which it is to be taken are announced at the meeting at which it is demanded. In any other case at least seven clear days' notice shall be given specifying the time and place at which the poll is to be taken.

53. A resolution in writing executed by or on behalf of each member who would have been entitled to vote upon it if it had been proposed at a general meeting at which he was present shall be as effectual as if it had been passed at a general meeting duly convened and held and may consist of several instruments in the like form each executed by or on behalf of one or more members.

Votes of members

54. Subject to any rights or restrictions attached to any shares, on a show of hands every member who (being an individual) is present in person or (being a corporation) is present by a duly authorised representative, not being himself a member entitled to vote, shall have one vote and on a poll every member shall have one vote for every share of which he is the holder.

55. In the case of joint holders the vote of the senior who tenders a vote, whether in person or by proxy, shall be accepted to the exclusion of the votes of the other joint holders; and seniority shall be determined by the order in which the names of the holders stand in the register of members.

56. A member in respect of whom an order has been made by any court having jurisdiction (whether in the United Kingdom or elsewhere) in matters concerning mental disorder may vote, whether on a show of hands or on a poll, by his receiver, curator bonis or other person authorised in that behalf appointed by that court, and any such receiver, curator bonis or other person may, on a poll, vote by proxy. Evidence to the satisfaction of the directors of the authority of the person claiming to exercise the right to vote shall be deposited at the office, or at such other place as is specified in accordance with the articles for the deposit of instruments of proxy, not less than 48 hours before the time appointed for hold-

ing the meeting or adjourned meeting at which the right to vote is to be exercised and in default the right to vote shall not be exercisable.

57. No member shall vote at any general meeting or at any separate meeting of the holders of any class of shares in the company, either in person or by proxy, in respect of any share held by him unless all moneys presently payable by him in respect of that share have been paid.

58. No objection shall be raised to the qualification of any voter except at the meeting or adjourned meeting at which the vote objected to is tendered, and every vote not disallowed at the meeting shall be valid. Any objection made in due time shall be referred to the chairman whose decision shall be final and conclusive.

59. On a poll votes may be given either personally or by proxy. A member may appoint more than one proxy to attend on the same occasion.

60. An instrument appointing a proxy shall be in writing, executed by or on behalf of the appointor and shall be in the following form (or in a form as near thereto as circumstances allow or in any other form which is usual or which the directors may approve)

" _____ PLC/Limited

I/We, _____ ,
of _____ ,
being a member/members of the above-named company, hereby appoint

_____
of _____ ,
or failing him/her, _____
of _____ ,
as my/our proxy to vote in my/our name(s) and on my/our behalf at the annual/extraordinary general meeting of the company to be held on _____ , and at any adjournment thereof.

Signed _____ on _____ _____ ."

61. Where it is desired to afford members an opportunity of instructing the proxy how he shall act the instrument appointing a proxy shall be in the following form (or in a form as near thereto as circumstances allow or in any other form which is usual or which the directors may approve) -

" _____ PLC/Limited

I/We, _____ ,
of _____ ,
being a member/members of the above-named company, hereby appoint

_____
of _____ ,
or failing him/her, _____
of _____ ,
as my/our proxy to vote in my/our name(s) and on my/our behalf at the annual/extraordinary general meeting of the company to be held on _____ , and at any adjournment thereof.

This form is to be used in respect of the resolutions mentioned below as follows:

Resolution No. 1 *for *against
Resolution No. 2 *for *against   * *Strike out whichever is not desired*

Unless otherwise instructed, the proxy may vote as he thinks fit or abstain from voting.

Signed _____ this day of _____ _____."

62. The instrument appointing a proxy and any authority under which it is executed or a copy of such authority certified notarially or in some other way approved by the directors may

(a) be deposited at the office or at such other place within the United Kingdom as is specified in the notice convening the meeting or in any instrument of proxy sent out by the company in relation to the meeting not less than forty-eight hours before the time for holding the meeting or adjourned meeting at which the person named in the instrument proposes to vote; or

(b) in the case of a poll taken more than forty-eight hours after it is demanded, be deposited as aforesaid after the poll has been demanded and not less than twenty-four hours before the time appointed for the taking of the poll; or

(c) where the poll is not taken forthwith but is taken not more than forty-eight hours after it was demanded, be delivered at the meeting at which the poll was demanded to the chairman or to the secretary or to any director; and an instrument of proxy which is not deposited or delivered in a manner so permitted shall be invalid.

63. A vote given or poll demanded by proxy or by the duly authorised representative of a corporation shall be valid notwithstanding the previous determination of the authority of the person voting or demanding a poll unless notice of the determination was received by the company at the office or at such other place at which the instrument of proxy was duly deposited before the commencement of the meeting or adjourned meeting at which the vote is given or the poll demanded or (in the case of a poll taken otherwise than on the same day as the meeting or adjourned meeting) the time appointed for taking the poll.

Number of directors

64. Unless otherwise determined by ordinary resolution, the number of directors (other than alternate directors) shall not be subject to any maximum but shall be not less than two.

Alternate directors

65. Any director (other than an alternate director) may appoint any other director, or any other person approved by resolution of the directors and willing to act, to be an alternate director and may remove from office an alternate director so appointed by him.

66. An alternate director shall be entitled to receive notice of all meetings of directors and of all meetings of committees of directors of which his appointor is a member, to attend and vote at any such meeting at which the director appointing him is not personally present, and generally to perform all the functions of his appointor as a director in his absence but shall not be entitled to receive any remuneration from the company for his services as an alternate director. But it shall not be necessary to give notice of such a meeting to an alternate director who is absent from the United Kingdom.

67. An alternate director shall cease to be an alternate director if his appointor ceases to be a director; but, if a director retires by rotation or otherwise but is re-appointed or deemed to have been re-appointed at the meeting at which he retires, any appointment of an alternate director made by him which was in force immediately prior to his retirement shall continue after his re-appointment.

68. Any appointment or removal of an alternate director shall be by notice to the company signed by the director making or revoking the appointment or in any other manner approved by the directors.

69. Save as otherwise provided in the articles, an alternate director shall be deemed for all purposes to be a director and shall alone be responsible for his own acts and defaults and he shall not be deemed to be the agent of the director appointing him.

Powers of directors

70. Subject to the provisions of the Act, the memorandum and the articles and to any directions given by special resolution, the business of the company shall be managed by the directors who may exercise all the powers of the company.

    No alteration of the memorandum or articles and no such direction shall invalidate any prior act of the directors which would have been valid if that alteration had not been made or that direction had not been given. The powers given by this regulation shall not be limited by any special power given to the directors by the articles and a meeting of directors at which a quorum is present may exercise all powers exercisable by the directors.

71. The directors may, by power of attorney or otherwise, appoint any person to be the agent of the company for such purposes and on such conditions as they determine, including authority for the agent to delegate all or any of his powers.

Delegation of directors' powers

72. The directors may delegate any of their powers to any committee consisting of one or more directors. They may also delegate to any managing director or any director holding any other executive office such of their powers as they consider desirable to be exercised by him. Any such delegation may be made subject to any conditions the directors may impose, and either collaterally with or to the exclusion of their own powers and may be revoked or altered. Subject to any such conditions, the proceedings of a committee with two or more members shall be governed by the articles regulating the proceedings of directors so far as they are capable of applying.

Appointment and retirement of directors

73. At the first annual general meeting all the directors shall retire from office, and at every subsequent annual general meeting one-third of the directors who are subject to retirement by rotation or, if their number is not three or a multiple of three, the number nearest to one-third shall retire from office; but, if there is only one director who is subject to retirement by rotation, he shall retire.

74. Subject to the provisions of the Act, the directors to retire by rotation shall be

those who have been longest in office since their last appointment or re-appointment, but as between persons who became or were last re-appointed directors on the same day those to retire shall (unless they otherwise agree among themselves) be determined by lot.

75.   If the company, at the meeting at which a director retires by rotation, does not fill the vacancy the retiring director shall, if willing to act, be deemed to have been re-appointed unless at the meeting it is resolved not to fill the vacancy or unless a resolution for the re-appointment of the director is put to the meeting and lost.

76.   No person other than a director retiring by rotation shall be appointed or re-appointed a director at any general meeting unless -

(a)   he is recommended by the directors; or

(b)   not less than fourteen nor more than thirty-five clear days before the date appointed for the meeting, notice executed by a member qualified to vote at the meeting has been given to the company of the intention to propose that person for appointment or re-appointment stating the particulars which would, if he were so appointed or re-appointed, be required to be included in the company's register of directors together with notice executed by that person of his willingness to be appointed or re-appointed.

77.   Not less than seven nor more than twenty-eight clear days before the date appointed for holding a general meeting notice shall be given to all who are entitled to receive notice of the meeting of any person (other than a director retiring by rotation at the meeting) who is recommended by the directors for appointment or re-appointment as a director at the meeting or in respect of whom notice has been duly given to the company of the intention to propose him at the meeting for appointment or re-appointment as a director. The notice shall give the particulars of that person which would, if he were so appointed or re-appointed, be required to be included in the company's register of directors.

78.   Subject as aforesaid, the company may by ordinary resolution appoint a person who is willing to act to be a director either to fill a vacancy or as an additional director and may also determine the rotation in which any additional directors are to retire.

79.   The directors may appoint a person who is willing to act to be a director, either to fill a vacancy or as an additional director, provided that the appointment does not cause the number of directors to exceed any number fixed by or in accordance with the articles as the maximum number of directors. A director so appointed shall hold office only until the next following annual general meeting and shall not be taken into account in determining the directors who are to retire by rotation at the meeting. If not re-appointed at such annual general meeting, he shall vacate office at the conclusion thereof.

80.   Subject as aforesaid, a director who retires at an annual general meeting may, if willing to act, be re-appointed. If he is not re-appointed, he shall retain office until the meeting appoints someone in his place, or if it does not do so, until the end of the meeting.

Disqualification and removal of directors

81.   The office of a director shall be vacated if -

(a) he ceases to be a director by virtue of any provision of the Act or he becomes prohibited by law from being a director; or

(b) he becomes bankrupt or makes any arrangement or composition with his creditors generally; or

(c) he is, or may be, suffering from mental disorder and either -

  (i) he is admitted to hospital in pursuance of an application for admission for treatment under the Mental Health Act 1983 or, in Scotland, an application for admission under the Mental Health (Scotland) Act 1960, or

  (ii) an order is made by a court having jurisdiction (whether in the United Kingdom or elsewhere) in matters concerning mental disorder for his detention or for the appointment of a receiver, curator bonis or other person to exercise powers with respect to his property or affairs; or

(d) he resigns his office by notice to the company; or

(e) he shall for more than six consecutive months have been absent without permission of the directors from meetings of directors held during that period and the directors resolve that his office be vacated.

Remuneration of directors

82. The directors shall be entitled to such remuneration as the company may by ordinary resolution determine and, unless the resolution provides otherwise, the remuneration shall be deemed to accrue from day to day.

Directors' expenses

83. The directors may be paid all travelling, hotel, and other expenses properly incurred by them in connection with their attendance at meetings of directors or committees of directors or general meetings or separate meetings of the holders of any class of shares or of debentures of the company or otherwise in connection with the discharge of their duties.

Directors' appointments and interests

84. Subject to the provisions of the Act, the directors may appoint one or more of their number to the office of managing director or to any other executive office under the company and may enter into an agreement or arrangement with any director for his employment by the company or for the provision by him of any services outside the scope of the ordinary duties of a director. Any such appointment, agreement or arrangement may be made upon such terms as the directors determine and they may remunerate any such director for his services as they think fit. Any appointment of a director to an executive office shall terminate if he ceases to be a director but without prejudice to any claim to damages for breach of the contract of service between the director and the company. A managing director and a director holding any other executive office shall not be subject to retirement by rotation.

85. Subject to the provisions of the Act, and provided that he has disclosed to the directors the nature and extent of any material interest of his, a director notwithstanding his office -

(a) may be a party to, or otherwise interested in, any transaction or arrangement with the company or in which the company is otherwise interested;

(b) may be a director or other officer of, or employed by, or a party to any transaction or arrangement with, or otherwise interested in, any body corporate promoted by the company or in which the company is otherwise interested; and

(c) shall not, by reason of his office, be accountable to the company for any benefit which he derives from any such office or employment or from any such transaction or arrangement or from any interest in any such body corporate and no such transaction or arrangement shall be liable to be avoided on the ground of any such interest or benefit.

86. For the purposes of regulation 85 -

(a) a general notice given to the directors that a director is to be regarded as having an interest of the nature and extent specified in the notice in any transaction or arrangement in which a specified person or class of persons is interested shall be deemed to be a disclosure that the director has an interest in any such transaction of the nature and extent so specified; and

(b) an interest of which a director has no knowledge and of which it is unreasonable to expect him to have knowledge shall not be treated as an interest of his.

Directors' gratuities and pensions

87. The directors may provide benefits, whether by the payment of gratuities or pensions or by insurance or otherwise, for any director who has held but no longer holds any executive office or employment with the company or with any body corporate which is or has been a subsidiary of the company or a predecessor in business of the company or of any such subsidiary, and for any member of his family (including a spouse and a former spouse) or any person who is or was dependent on him, and may (as well before as after he ceases to hold such office or employment) contribute to any fund and pay premiums for the purchase or provision of any such benefit.

Proceedings of directors

88. Subject to the provisions of the articles, the directors may regulate their proceedings as they think fit. A director may, and the secretary at the request of a director shall, call a meeting of the directors. It shall not be necessary to give notice of a meeting to a director who is absent from the United Kingdom. Questions arising at a meeting shall be decided by a majority of votes. In the case of an equality of votes, the chairman shall have a second or casting vote. A director who is also an alternate director shall be entitled in the absence of his appointor to a separate vote on behalf of his appointor in addition to his own vote.

89. The quorum for the transaction of the business of the directors may be fixed by the directors and unless so fixed at any other number shall be two. A person who holds office only as an alternate director shall, if his appointor is not present, be counted in the quorum.

90. The continuing directors or a sole continuing director may act notwithstanding any vacancies in their number, but, if the number of directors is less than the

number fixed as the quorum, the continuing directors or director may act only for the purpose of filling vacancies or of calling a general meeting.

91.   The directors may appoint one of their number to be the chairman of the board of directors and may at any time remove him from that office. Unless he is unwilling to do so, the director so appointed shall preside at every meeting of directors at which he is present. But if there is no director holding that office, or if the director holding it is unwilling to preside or is not present within five minutes after the time appointed for the meeting, the directors present may appoint one of their number to be chairman of the meeting.

92.   All acts done by a meeting of directors, or of a committee of directors, or by a person acting as a director shall, notwithstanding that it be afterwards discovered that there was a defect in the appointment of any director or that any of them were disqualified from holding office, or had vacated office, or were not entitled to vote, be as valid as if every such person had been duly appointed and was qualified and had continued to be a director and had been entitled to vote.

93.   A resolution in writing signed by all the directors entitled to receive notice of a meeting of directors or of a committee of directors shall be as valid and effectual as if it had been passed at a meeting of directors or (as the case may be) a committee of directors duly convened and held and may consist of several documents in the like form each signed by one or more directors; but a resolution signed by an alternate director need not also be signed by his appointor and, if it is signed by a director who has appointed an alternate director, it need not be signed by the alternate director in that capacity.

94.   Save as otherwise provided by the articles, a director shall not vote at a meeting of directors or of a committee of directors on any resolution concerning a matter in which he has, directly or indirectly, an interest or duty which is material and which conflicts or may conflict with the interests of the company unless his interest or duty arises only because the case falls within one or more of the following paragraphs -

(a)   the resolution relates to the giving to him of a guarantee, security, or indemnity in respect of money lent to, or an obligation incurred by him for the benefit of, the company or any of its subsidiaries;

(b)   the resolution relates to the giving to a third party of a guarantee, security, or indemnity in respect of an obligation of the company or any of its subsidiaries for which the director has assumed responsibility in whole or part and whether alone or jointly with others under a guarantee or indemnity or by the giving of security;

(c)   his interest arises by virtue of his subscribing or agreeing to subscribe for any shares, debentures or other securities of the company or any of its subsidiaries, or by virtue of his being, or intending to become, a participant in the underwriting or sub-underwriting of an offer of any such shares, debentures, or other securities by the company or any of its subsidiaries for subscription, purchase or exchange;

(d)   the resolution relates in any way to a retirement benefits scheme which has been approved, or is conditional upon approval, by the Board of Inland Revenue for taxation purposes.

For the purposes of this regulation, an interest of a person who is, for any purpose of the Act (excluding any statutory modification thereof not in force when this regulation becomes binding on the company), connected with a director shall be treated as an interest of the director and, in relation to an alternate director, an interest of his appointor shall be treated as an interest of the alternate director without prejudice to any interest which the alternate director has otherwise.

95. A director shall not be counted in the quorum present at a meeting in relation to a resolution on which he is not entitled to vote.

96. The company may by ordinary resolution suspend or relax to any extent, either generally or in respect of any particular matter, any provision of the articles prohibiting a director from voting at a meeting of directors or of a committee of directors.

97. Where proposals are under consideration concerning the appointment of two or more directors to offices or employments with the company or any body corporate in which the company is interested the proposals may be divided and considered in relation to each director separately and (provided he is not for another reason precluded from voting) each of the directors concerned shall be entitled to vote and be counted in the quorum in respect of each resolution except that concerning his own appointment.

98. If a question arises at a meeting of directors or of a committee of directors as to the right of a director to vote, the question may, before the conclusion of the meeting, be referred to the chairman of the meeting and his ruling in relation to any director other than himself shall be final and conclusive.

Secretary

99. Subject to the provisions of the Act, the secretary shall be appointed by the directors for such term, at such remuneration and upon such conditions as they may think fit; and any secretary so appointed may be removed by them.

Minutes

100. The directors shall cause minutes to be made in books kept for the purpose -

   (a) of all appointments of officers made by the directors; and

   (b) of all proceedings at meetings of the company, of the holders of any class of shares in the company, and of the directors, and of committees of directors, including the names of the directors present at each such meeting.

The seal

101. The seal shall only be used by the authority of the directors or of a committee of directors authorised by the directors. The directors may determine who shall sign any instrument to which the seal is affixed and unless otherwise so determined it shall be signed by a director and by the secretary or by a second director.

Dividends

102. Subject to the provisions of the Act, the company may by ordinary resolution declare dividends in accordance with the respective rights of the members, but

no dividend shall exceed the amount recommended by the directors.

103. Subject to the provisions of the Act, the directors may pay interim dividends if it appears to them that they are justified by the profits of the company available for distribution. If the share capital is divided into different classes, the directors may pay interim dividends on shares which confer deferred or non-preferred rights with regard to dividend as well as on shares which confer preferential rights with regard to dividend, but no interim dividend shall be paid on shares carrying deferred or non-preferred rights if, at the time of payment, any preferential dividend is in arrear. The directors may also pay at intervals settled by them any dividend payable at a fixed rate if it appears to them that the profits available for distribution justify the payment. Provided the directors act in good faith they shall not incur any liability to the holders of shares conferring preferred rights for any loss they may suffer by the lawful payment of an interim dividend on any shares having deferred or non-preferred rights.

104. Except as otherwise provided by the rights attached to shares, all dividends shall be declared and paid according to the amounts paid up on the shares on which the dividend is paid. All dividends shall be apportioned and paid proportionately to the amounts paid up on the shares during any portion or portions of the period in respect of which the dividend is paid; but, if any share is issued on terms providing that it shall rank for dividend as from a particular date, that share shall rank for dividend accordingly.

105. A general meeting declaring a dividend may, upon the recommendation of the directors, direct that it shall be satisfied wholly or partly by the distribution of assets and, where any difficulty arises in regard to the distribution, the directors may settle the same and in particular may issue fractional certificates and fix the value for distribution of any assets and may determine that cash shall be paid to any member upon the footing of the value so fixed in order to adjust the rights of members and may vest any assets in trustees.

106. Any dividend or other moneys payable in respect of a share may be paid by cheque sent by post to the registered address of the person entitled or, if two or more persons are the holders of the share or are jointly entitled to it by reason of the death or bankruptcy of the holder, to the registered address of that one of those persons who is first named in the register of members or to such person and to such address as the person or persons entitled may in writing direct. Every cheque shall be made payable to the order of the person or persons entitled or to such other person as the person or persons entitled may in writing direct and payment of the cheque shall be a good discharge to the company. Any joint holder or other person jointly entitled to a share as aforesaid may give receipts for any dividend or other moneys payable in respect of the share.

107. No dividend or other moneys payable in respect of a share shall bear interest against the company unless otherwise provided by the rights attached to the share.

108. Any dividend which has remained unclaimed for twelve years from the date when it became due for payment shall, if the directors so resolve, be forfeited and cease to remain owing by the company.

Accounts

109. No member shall (as such) have any right of inspecting any accounting records or other book or document of the company except as conferred by statute or

authorised by the directors or by ordinary resolution of the company.

Capitalisation of profits

110. The directors may with the authority of an ordinary resolution of the company -

(a) subject as hereinafter provided, resolve to capitalise any undivided profits of the company not required for paying any preferential dividend (whether or not they are available for distribution) or any sum standing to the credit of the company's share premium account or capital redemption reserve;

(b) appropriate the sum resolved to be capitalised to the members who would have been entitled to it if it were distributed by way of dividend and in the same proportions and apply such sum on their behalf either in or towards paying up the amounts, if any, for the time being unpaid on any shares held by them respectively, or in paying up in full unissued shares or debentures of the company of a nominal amount equal to that sum, and allot the shares or debentures credited as fully paid to those members, or as they may direct, in those proportions, or partly in one way and partly in the other: but the share premium account, the capital redemption reserve, and any profits which are not available for distribution may, for the purposes of this regulation, only be applied in paying up unissued shares to be allotted to members credited as fully paid;

(c) make such provision by the issue of fractional certificates or by payment in cash or otherwise as they determine in the case of shares or debentures becoming distributable under this regulation in fractions; and

(d) authorise any person to enter on behalf of all the members concerned into an agreement with the company providing for the allotment to them respectively, credited as fully paid, of any shares or debentures to which they are entitled upon such capitalisation, any agreement made under such authority being binding on all such members.

Notices

111. Any notice to be given to or by any person pursuant to the articles shall be in writing except that a notice calling a meeting of the directors need not be in writing.

112. The company may give any such notice to a member either personally or by sending it by post in a prepaid envelope addressed to the member at his registered address or by leaving it at that address. In the case of joint holders of a share, all notices shall be given to the joint holder whose name stands first in the register of members in respect of the joint holding and notice so given shall be sufficient notice to all the joint holders. A member whose registered address is not within the United Kingdom and who gives to the company an address within the United Kingdom at which notices may be given to him shall be entitled to have notices given to him at that address, but otherwise no such member shall be entitled to receive any notice from the company.

113. A member present, either in person or by proxy, at any meeting of the company or of the holders of any class of shares in the company shall be deemed to have received notice of the meeting and, where requisite, of the purposes for which it was called.

114. Every person who becomes entitled to a share shall be bound by any notice in respect of that share which, before his name is entered in the register of members, has been duly given to a person from whom he derives his title.

115. Proof that an envelope containing a notice was properly addressed, prepaid and posted shall be conclusive evidence that the notice was given. A notice shall be deemed to be given at the expiration of forty-eight hours after the envelope containing it was posted.

116. A notice may be given by the company to the persons entitled to a share in consequence of the death or bankruptcy of a member by sending or delivering it, in any manner authorised by the articles for the giving of notice to a member, addressed to them by name, or by the title of representatives of the deceased, or trustee of the bankrupt or by any like description at the address, if any, within the United Kingdom supplied for that purpose by the persons claiming to be so entitled. Until such an address has been supplied, a notice may be given in any manner in which it might have been given if the death or bankruptcy had not occurred.

Winding up

117. If the company is wound up, the liquidator may, with the sanction of an extraordinary resolution of the company and any other sanction required by the Act, divide among the members in specie the whole or any part of the assets of the company and may, for that purpose, value any assets and determine how the division shall be carried out as between the members or different classes of members. The liquidator may, with the like sanction, vest the whole or any part of the assets in trustees upon such trusts for the benefit of the members as he with the like sanction determines, but no member shall be compelled to accept any assets upon which there is a liability.

Indemnity

118. Subject to the provisions of the Act but without prejudice to any indemnity to which a director may otherwise be entitled, every director or other officer or auditor of the company shall be indemnified out of the assets of the company against any liability incurred by him in defending any proceedings, whether civil or criminal, in which judgment is given in his favour or in which he is acquitted or in connection with any application in which relief is granted to him by the court from liability for negligence, default, breach of duty or breach of trust in relation to the affairs of the company.